Praise 1

A FUNNY THING
GYNECOLOGI(
KETTERING C,

"A daring romantic comedy . . . Feiffer is c...
—Charles McNulty, *Los Angeles Times*

"*Funny Thing* makes a convincing case that hard laughter is an absolutely appropriate response to those moments when life seems like too bad a joke not to respond otherwise . . . an exposed nerve of a script."
—Ben Brantley, *The New York Times*

"Feiffer's work always has guts . . . powerful . . . But for all the farcical, caustic humor in the piece, this lovely play really is about a coming together in the spirit of shared humanity."
—Chris Jones, *Chicago Tribune*

I'M GONNA PRAY FOR YOU SO HARD

"Viciously funny . . . brutally effective. Feiffer takes a tough look at the forces that can bring us to our knees."
—Adam Feldman, *Time Out New York*

"A bone-chilling . . . punishing drama."
—Charles Isherwood, *The New York Times*

"Blistering, blackly funny."
—Joe Dziemianowicz, *New York Daily News*

"One minute you're laughing, the next you're cringing . . . the play sticks in your head like a crazy nightmare."
—Elisabeth Vincentelli, *New York Post*

"Funny, scary, and completely over the top in its own right . . . goes straight for the jugular through the heart." —Robert Hofler, *The Wrap*

"Provocative, sensitive, shocking and often very unsettling . . . polished and probing. One of the best plays I've seen this season."
—Rex Reed, *New York Observer*

"Exhilaratingly toxic." —Joe McGovern, *Entertainment Weekly*

"A hard-hearted stunner." —Michael Schulman, *The New Yorker*

"Halley Feiffer's ferocious, explosive dialogue in *I'm Gonna Pray For You So Hard* is in a class of its own." —Lee Kinney, *TheEasy.com*

"It's a fearless piece of work, riveting and hilarious."
—Robert Feldberg, *Bergen Record*

HOW TO MAKE FRIENDS AND THEN KILL THEM

"Ms. Feiffer . . . is building a reputation for fearlessness."
                              —Neil Genzlinger, *The New York Times*

"Thank God . . . for the warped creative mind of playwright/actress Halley Feiffer, who harnesses the weird to full, gory effect in *How to Make Friends and Then Kill Them,* an uproarious and deeply unsettling new dark comedy . . . Equally laugh-out-loud funny, jaw-droppingly gross, and thoroughly sad . . . Feiffer's unique, refreshing voice is one to which attention should be paid."   —David Gordon, *Theatermania*

"Disturbingly funny."   —Joe Dziemianowicz, *New York Daily News*

"Feiffer . . . has a commendable eye for the absurd."
                                             —*The New Yorker*

"A wicked comedy . . . Feiffer . . . is an expert comic actor with an appealingly skewed sensibility." —Elisabeth Vincentelli, *New York Post*

"There's great stuff here . . . dark and weird."
                              —Helen Shaw, *Time Out New York*

HALLEY FEIFFER is a writer and actress. Plays include *I'm Gonna Pray For You So Hard* (World Premiere Atlantic Theater Company, Outer Critics Circle Nomination), *Moscow Moscow Moscow Moscow Moscow Moscow* (World Premiere Williamstown Theatre Festival, MCC Theater), *How To Make Friends and Then Kill Them* (World Premiere Rattlestick Playwrights Theatre), *The Pain of My Belligerence* (World Premiere Playwrights Horizons) and this play (World Premiere MCC Theater), the West Coast premiere of which she starred in at the Geffen Playhouse. Her plays have been produced around the country and in the UK. Acting credits include the Broadway revivals of *The Front Page* and *The House of Blue Leaves* (Theatre World Award) and numerous off-Broadway productions including *Tigers Be Still* (Roundabout, Drama League Nom.). TV & film includes recurring roles on HBO's *Mildred Piece* and *Bored to Death* and the films *The Squid and the Whale*, *Gentlemen Broncos* and *He's Way More Famous than You*, which she also co-wrote. TV writing credits include *The One Percent* (Starz), Purity (Showtime), *Mozart in the Jungle* (Amazon) and original pilots for FX and TNT. She is a producer on the Showtime series *Kidding*, starring Jim Carrey.

ALSO BY HALLEY FEIFFER

How To Make Friends and Then Kill Them
I'm Gonna Pray For You So Hard

A Funny Thing Happened On the Way to the Gynecologic Oncology Unit At Memorial Sloan Kettering Cancer Center of New York City

A PLAY BY

Halley Feiffer

THE OVERLOOK PRESS
New York, NY

This edition first published in the United States in 2018 by
The Overlook Press, Peter Mayer Publishers, Inc.

141 Wooster Street
New York, NY 10012
www.overlookpress.com
For bulk and special sales, please contact sales@overlookny.com,
or write us at above address.

Cataloging-in-Publication Data is available from the Library of Congress

Book design and type formatting by Bernard Schleifer
Manufactured in the United States of America
ISBN 978-1-4683-1551-6
3 5 7 9 10 8 6 4 2

*A Funny Thing Happened
On the Way to the Gynecologic
Oncology Unit At Memorial
Sloan Kettering Cancer Center
of New York City*

PREFACE

It's technically spring but it feels like winter. That terrible time of year when the holiday decorations are long since gone and the ever-increasing afternoon light fools you into feeling hopeful that the blood-chilling cold will fade overnight like magic, as it sometimes does. But it hasn't yet. And I'm home from college — not because I'm on break, but because my mother has cancer.

I'm twenty-one years old. Emotionally, I'm . . . oh, eleven? I don't know it yet but I'm an alcoholic. (I'll make this fun discovery and get sober three years later.) At this point, I'm drinking a bottle of cheap wine by myself every night just to make the very cruel voices in my head go to sleep. Luckily, I fall asleep with them. I wake up every morning and the voices are back. Luckily, I know I can drink again that night. It's a good system, I think. Or, good enough. Reliable, anyway. Oh, who am I kidding? It's all I know.

I'm in an impressive amount of denial about how unhealthy I am, how basically doomed I am, how I'm swapping out my dreams for $7 lukewarm rosé that comes in a box. (Don't knock it 'til you've tried it!) (Actually, knock it — don't try it.)

My mother has the best sense of humor of anyone I know — an uncanny ability to find the funny in almost any situation, the darker the better. One time she threw a *Stalag 17* theme party. No occasion — she just loves the movie *Stalag 17*. She made a cake with a POW camp on top, complete with barbed wire and little toy soldiers standing guard as other toy soldiers try to scale the fence and escape into war-ridden Germany. She invited her friends and my friends. Our friends were confused. Mom and I yucked it up.

But Mom isn't laughing now. She's asleep in her hospital bed. I'm glad she's asleep. She's exhausted. She's had an awful week: a hysterectomy a few days ago to treat cervical cancer, which unex-pectedly revealed masses of ovarian cancer, too. We're waiting for more tests results, to determine essentially what kind of life Mom will lead from here on out: one in which she'll have to succumb to vicious rounds of treatment to end up ultimately very likely okay — or one in which she will have to start saying her goodbyes.

I've taken the bus over here from the apartment I grew up in on the Upper West Side, every morning since the procedure. I try to arrive early, since my mother told me they wake her up around five. I stay with her until she falls asleep. My sister is still a kid — ten years younger than me — and my father is charged with caring for her while I care for Mom. I am trying to be helpful, however I can be. And I don't know how I can be. Because the only tool I have for soothing myself is $7 box-wine rosé.

What's that? My mother's roommate on the other side of the curtain. What is she saying? Muttering in her sleep. The painkillers make her somewhat delirious, I think. She's in worse shape than Mom. She's older — maybe seventy. Bald, from chemo. Years of it, maybe. Alone. Where's her family? No one's visited her yet, the entire time I've been here. Maybe she's been here so long — maybe in and out, so many times — that they've all grown tired of coming. How sad. I don't know. I'm just making stuff up. Mom is sleeping, and I'm thinking of stories. I wish I could actually write down stories. But I can't. Because I'm drunk or hung over all of the time.

A noise — a voice, on the other side of the curtain. A nurse? A visitor! The roommate *does* have a family. Could it be — what if it's — oh God, wouldn't it be funny— am I a terrible person if I — oh God, *I wish it were her son!* Her cute, college-age son — maybe older — just a bit older — someone I could flirt with — sneak off with — kiss a little bit, even, in the handicap bathroom! And then —

What's wrong with you?

The voice in my head. The cruel one — one of them, anyway. Only this time I can't make it go away. Because there's no rosé here. There's just me and Mom.

What *is* wrong with me? What am I doing? Sitting here in a visitor's chair at Memorial Sloan Kettering Cancer Center, looking at my sleeping mother — so pale and small in her wrinkled hospital gown — fantasizing about having an affair with the imaginary son of my mother's roommate in the oncology ward.

I'm sick.

I hate myself. I listen to the voices on the other side of the curtain while I sit here, hating myself. It is the roommate's son, I think — but he doesn't sound cute at all. He sounds old. Middle-aged. Angry. I don't want to have an affair with this guy. I just want to sit here, hating myself.

You're sick. The voice in my head is so mean! But it's right. But then —

Another voice. Again, in my head. But it's new — or maybe not new. Maybe old — but new to me, in a way, since I'm not used to it. Because it is so much quiet than the other one, than the very cruel voice — than all of the cruel ones. And it says: *You're sick, okay, but you're not bad. You're just scared, that's all. And that's okay.*

And it also says: *This would be a good premise for a play.*

And the other voice says: *We're not here to think of ideas for plays! We're here to take care of Mom.*

And the other voice says: *But maybe we can do both. Maybe Mom would want it that way.*

And the other voice says: *Who are we kidding? We don't even write plays!*

And the other voice says: *But maybe we can.*

And before the other voice, the cruel one — or one of the many cruel ones — can pipe up:

Mom's awake.

And I look at her. And I suddenly sort of know what to do.

This is a beautiful hospital — the walls are a soft pink, adorned with photographs and paintings of flowers so succulent you can almost smell them; but when you do inhale, it's the chemicals in the air you smell: the disinfectant, the metallic aftermath of so many drugs being pumped into so many veins, in so many rooms, all over this floor. And I know in this moment that my mom just wants company. That she just wants *my* company. That she just wants me. That even though I don't know how to soothe her, I do, sort of — because all I have to do is be with her. Is be myself. Because it's me that she loves — even if I do drink a bottle of rosé by myself every night and even if I do feel utterly unequipped to take care of her and even if I was just sitting here imagining a passionate embrace with a man who doesn't exist on the other side of this curtain so that I could escape this unbearably painful reality, *that's* the part of me that Mom loves most of all, maybe. Because that's the part of me that comes from her. The part that can find light — find the funny, even — in the most horrific of circumstances.

And maybe that's the part that I like, too.

"Do you want some water?" I ask my mom. She nods. And I bring her some. And turn on the TV. Our favorite show: *Law & Order: Special Victims Unit.* We take turns betting on which episode this one is (we've seen them all): the one where the AIDS patient screws half the men in New York City as part of a twisted plot to spew disease to the farthest corners of the earth? The one where the young woman with Down syndrome is forced to have sex with her boss when he tells her it's "exercise"? The one where —

Oh my, and now we're laughing! We're laughing, here in the hospital. On the other side of the curtain, the roommate and son get quiet. *What are they laughing about?* They might be thinking. Or maybe not. Maybe the roommate has fallen asleep. Maybe the son is fantasizing about having an affair with me! Probably not. Probably he's not that fucked up. Probably that's just me. And probably that's okay.

And Mom and I are still laughing. And we watch *Law & Order.* A commercial comes on. Mom dozes off again; the sun starts to fade. I don't like the darkness — it makes me want to drink. But at least the sun is setting later and later these days. And even though it doesn't feel like it, soon I know that it will be spring. And Mom won't be in the hospital forever. And if we're lucky, she won't have cancer forever. And maybe I won't be sick forever, either — with whatever it is that's wrong with me. And maybe, *maybe,* I can even —

It's back! *SVU.* I watch, while Mom sleeps. And I reach out. And I hold her hand.

—Halley Feiffer, February 2018

PRODUCTION CREDITS

A Funny Thing Happened On the Way To the Gynecologic Oncology Unit at Memorial Sloan Kettering Cancer Center of New York City by Halley Feiffer had its world premiere at MCC Theater June 2, 2016. Artistic Directors: Robert LuPone, Bernard Telsey, & William Cantler Executive Director: Blake West
It was directed by Trip Cullman.

CAST

KARLA	Beth Behrs
MARCIE	Lisa Emery
DON	Erik Lochtefeld
GEENA	Jacqueline Sydney

CHARACTERS

KARLA: A charismatic woman in her early thirties whose pretty face and somewhat childlike demeanor belies an incredibly dirty mouth and mind. Spunky, spirited, angry, wickedly funny. A stand-up comedian with a real penchant for dark humor which she uses to hide behind and distract herself from the pain of her mother's sickness.

DON: An unassuming man in his late forties. The kind of person who you would never even notice on the subway or walking down the street—an "everyman" in the most boring sense of the word. Clearly has been through a lot of stress both in life-in-general and also more acutely quite recently. Employs a raging temper to mask the gaping wound left from his recent marital split and his mother's illness.

MARCIE: Karla's mother. A painfully thin, pale, dyed-redhead in her fifties. Recovering from a hysterectomy that she had to treat her Stage I endometrial cancer. Very dry wit, like Karla. In her case, her dark humor belies not only oceans of pain but also an abusive, selfish cruelty. Still, she is capable of deep love and moments of tender vulnerability.

GEENA: Don's mother. A heavyset woman in her sixties who hasn't paid attention to her personal appearance in about forty years. Has been battling ovarian cancer for seven years. Brave. Tired.

SETTING

A hospital room in New York City.

NOTES

A "/" indicates overlapping dialogue.

A ". . ." does not necessarily indicate a pause. Rather, it connotes a sort of shift in thought—a momentary, often almost unrecognizable jump, snag or tangle in communication.

Beats can be very quick—they need not linger, unless otherwise indicated.

SCENE 1

A hospital room in New York City.

The decor makes every effort to be cheery: the walls are painted a pretty, soft pink, and there is a large and festive portrait of a somewhat yonic flower mounted over each of the two beds. Still, it is a hospital room, and the thick plastic blinds that hang in the windows and obscure the lovely late-afternoon sunlight — coupled with the occasional beeping emitted intermittently from the IV stands — remind us that this is a place where cheeriness is, for the most part, put on hold.

The room's two beds are separated by a thick, plastic, pea-green curtain. The door to the room is on the SL side. The door to the bathroom is on the SR side; it is currently open, and we can see that the bathroom is large and handicap-accessible, complete with a sit-down shower. Each side of the room is equipped with a pitcher of water and a stack of Dixie cups. A TV hangs in front of each bed. There is a window in between the two beds, exposing the New York City skyline.

In the SL bed lies GEENA, *a heavyset woman in her sixties who hasn't paid attention to her personal appearance in about forty years. She is fast asleep; her face is scrunched up like a lemon — like she is worrying and fretting even in a state of deep unconsciousness.*

In the SR bed lies MARCIE, *a pale, painfully thin dyed-redhead in her late-fifties. She is also fast asleep. Her skeletal arm hangs off the side of the bed. She looks so slack and relaxed that we fear she may fall out of bed at any moment.*

Both women are hooked up to an IV drip, and both wear nasal cannulas to administer oxygen. Next to each bed is a bedstand and a not-very-comfortable-looking chair for visitors.

In the chair next to MARCIE*'s bed sits* KARLA. *She is a clearly intelligent, somewhat visibly-neurotic and quite charming woman in her early thirties, who at this moment seems a bit keyed up. She wears skinny jeans and sneakers and a colorful ironic sweater. She sips water from a Dixie cup and taps a red pen on a marble notebook that sits in her lap, covered with messy scrawl.*

KARLA *refers to her notes as she speaks to* MARCIE, *despite* MARCIE*'s being dead asleep.*

> KARLA

"I've been single for so long? I've started having sexual fantasies about my vibrator."

> MARCIE*'s mouth hangs open; she snores. Some drool begins to seep out.*

> KARLA

(Re: the drool.)

Oh. Um.

> KARLA *looks around, spots a box of tissues on the bedstand.*
>
> *She grabs a tissue and delicately wipes* MARCIE*'s mouth. Throws the tissue away.*

> KARLA

Now what do you think works better, "sexual fantasies" or "sex dreams"? Or *"wet dreams"?*

> MARCIE *emits a little groan in her sleep.*

> KARLA

I know. I actually think "wet dreams" is the funniest option, but I'm worried it might not get a laugh because girls don't have wet dreams.

> *(Considers this.)*

Per se. . . .

> MARCIE *emits a tiny, forceful snore.*

> KARLA

Yeah, fuck it. Wet dreams? You're in.

> *(Crosses something out and scribbles in her notebook.)*

And I have more stuff I could add on to it, too—like I could elaborate even more?

> MARCIE *emits a sort of shuddering, four-part, near-violent snore.*

KARLA

Ummm. . . .

KARLA *reaches out and gives her mom's arm a quick,*
. *somewhat awkward little rub. Then—she returns to her*
notes.

KARLA

Like I could—oh Idunno this is all just improv, but like I could be
like: "Instead of a strong, chiseled, oiled-up man throwing open my
bedroom door and raping me? I just have visions of like, my vibrator
standing in the archway, backlit by silvery moonlight, sometimes wearing a fedora (sometimes not), and lovingly fucking me 'til sunrise."
(Beat.)
What do you think of that? That was just improv.

MARCIE *starts to snore lightly, almost rhythmically.* KARLA
begins to chew her cuticles, absently, as she peruses her
notes.

KARLA

Maybe the rape part was a bit much.

KARLA *continues to chew her cuticles as she starts to*
scribble in her notebook.

DON *enters, quietly. He is an unassuming man in his late*
forties. His face is drawn, gray, pursed; he looks like he
has been through the wringer both in life-in-general and
also more acutely quite recently. He wears a corduroy
jacket with big holes in both elbows and a pair of extremely
depressing sweatpants.

He slips in silently and sits down next to GEENA*'s bed. Looks*
at GEENA. *His face fills with sadness. He reaches out and*
takes her hand, gives it a squeeze. Then, he leans back in his
chair, reaches into his jacket pocket and removes a copy
of The New Yorker. *He reads.*

On the other side of the curtain, KARLA *starts to talk again,*
oblivious.

KARLA

I don't know, I kinda don't think there's anything funnier than rape.

DON *reacts, with horror.*

A loud snore from MARCIE.

KARLA

Okay, well what if I just said something like . . .

(Reading from notes.)

"I'm in bed, dripping wet, waiting for my vibrator to come fuck me"?

On the other side of the curtain, DON *is becoming increasingly aghast.*

KARLA

Maybe that's like—does that kinda take the teeth out of it, though? Am I being a pussy? Arghhh, I can never tell if I'm just resorting to being a big, gaping wide *pussy.*

On the other side of the curtain, DON *thinks he is perhaps hallucinating.*

KARLA *scribbles in her notebook, then gets another idea.*

KARLA

Or I could even work the rape element *into* it, but in like a different way—like I could say something like: "I love getting fucked by my vibrator 'cause I know it'll never rape me."

(Thinks.)

Or something like that.

On the other side of the curtain, DON *has put his* New Yorker *down and is listening to* KARLA *with silent horror and fury.*

KARLA *continues, oblivious, to chew her cuticles, scribble, think, improvise. She laughs at something she just wrote down.*

KARLA

How about—ha ha—how about: "I only rape myself with my vibrator when I'm *really angry* at myself"?

MARCIE *snores.*

KARLA

Too much?

KARLA *chews a cuticle and scribbles.*

DON *'s face is, at this point, nearly crimson. He is shaking.*

KARLA

Okay here's a compromise: "I only play out my rape fantasies with my *vibrator,* 'cause I know it will always respect my safe word."

(Thinks.)

It's still maybe too vague. . . .

> *(Scribbles.)*

"It's so fun to get raped by your vibrator, 'cause—

DON

> *(Quiet, but forceful.)*

I'm sorry—I'm *sorry?*

> KARLA*'s eyes go wide. She panics. She had no idea* DON *was there. She chews her cuticles, fiercely.*
>
> *A long, long, deadly beat. Then—*

KARLA

> *(At a loss.)*

. . . yes . . .?

DON

> *(Trying very hard to convey a tone of equanimity.)*

Could you keep it *down?* Over there? / Could you—

KARLA

> *(Earnestly.)*

I didn't realize someone else was in here.

> DON *doesn't say anything. He just rubs his temples, hard. Inhales, sharply. Then—*
>
> *His cell phone suddenly VIBRATES, loudly. He takes it out of his pocket, reads something on it that is obviously displeasing to him, then puts the phone back in his pocket.*

KARLA

> *(Really softly,)*

I'll be more quiet. Sorry.

> KARLA *returns to her notes, and* MARCIE.

KARLA

> *(A whisper.)*

"It's so fun to get raped by your vibrator, 'cause you don't have to go to the police after, you can just—

> *(Thinks.)*

No . . .

> *(Scribbles; thinks.)*

"It's so fun to get raped by your vibr—

DON

(A harsh whisper.)

I'm *sorry?!*

> The rest of their conversation is spoken in low tones—
> often heated—but still, always relatively measured whis-
> pers, so as not to wake GEENA *and* MARCIE.

DON

I'm SORRY—what / are you—

KARLA

I'm being *quiet.*

DON

That's not . . . the *point!*

KARLA

Okay, well would you care to *illuminate* for me what you believe *"the point"* / to be . . .?

DON

The *point* is that you are not the only person in / this room.

KARLA

I *told* you I didn't realize someone else was / *in here* . . .!

DON

You didn't *"realize"* someone / else was *"in here"?!*

KARLA

No! I *told* you, I thought it was just me / and my—

DON

You didn't *"realize"* there was a sixty-five-year-old woman fighting with every fiber of her being to combat a rapacious case of ovarian cancer in here? You didn't / *"realize"* that?!

KARLA

Why are you *talking* to me / like this . . .?!

DON

Why am I *"talking"* to / you" like—

KARLA

Why are you talking to me like I'm some kind of fucking / idiot?!

DON

Why are you *acting* / like some kind of—

KARLA

You *told* me to be quiet and that's what I'm *fucking* / *doing!*

DON

Hey—language! / *Language!*

KARLA

What—"language"?! Are you my fucking / *pre-school teacher?!*

DON

We are in a *hospital!*

KARLA

I *noticed!!*

DON

There are *ladies* present!

KARLA

I'm a fucking lady!

DON

Oh, hah. / HAH!

KARLA

You don't know! You don't even know what I *look* like, 'cause you're not man enough to pull aside this fucking *curtain* and come over here and belittle me / to my face!

DON

(Incensed.)
Oh that's it. / That's *IT.*

KARLA

That's *what*? What are you / gonna do?

DON

I'm . . . getting a *nurse!*

KARLA

(Laughs, incredulous.)
You're "*getting a* / *nurse*"?!

DON
(Flustered.)
I'm—getting a—hospital / administrator. I'm—

KARLA
(Cruelly mocking him.)
"I'm calling *my mommy*—I'm *telling* on / you!

DON
I'm *sorry?* / I'm SORRY?

KARLA
Oh, I don't think you're "sorry"—I think you, my friend, are the *opposite* / of sorry.

DON
It's an *expression.* / Jesus!

KARLA
It's an "*expression*" that little *pansies* use, 'cause when you say—
(Cruel imitation.)
"I'm *sorry?*" "I'm SORRY?"
(Back to her voice.)
—what you're *really* saying is that you think *I* should be sorry. You say—
(Even crueller imitation.)
"*I'm sorry?! I'm SORRRY?!*"
(Back to her voice.)
—as a passive aggressive attempt to *control* me / and tell *me* what to say—

DON
Oh / I know *exactly* where this is going . . .

KARLA
—because even though you don't know me (I'm just a fucking plastic *curtain* to you), you can tell from the sound of my voice that I am a young *woman*—

DON
Yup! / *Heeere* we go. . . .

KARLA
—so in your terribly insecure / imagin*ation*—

DON

Are / you *always like* this? Do you have *friends?*

KARLA

—that signifies that you are in a position of *power* over me, an imagined fact that translates in your emasculated *fantasy*-brain to carte-blanche permission to fucking *talk* to me / any way you *feel* like, I guess, because—

DON

Dear / god what *happened* to you in your miserable *childhood* to make you *become* this person?!

KARLA

(Barreling through, ignoring of his interjections.)
—your terrifyingly immature sub*conscious* tells you that THAT is the *one way* you can feel *powerful* when you are in the midst of the most *castrating* powerlessness *of your life,* wherein your mother is dying of *cancer* over there and you are completely *powerless over THAT.*

A beat. DON *is stony-faced.*

KARLA's *eyes betray perhaps a hint of contrition—a nagging fear that she may have crossed a line.*

DON's *face gets kind strange—sort of pink, a little crinkly. Then—*

DON

(Cold as ice.)
You're a little *bitch*, you know that?

A beat. KARLA's *face turns crimson. She starts to shake— almost imperceptibly. Then—*

KARLA

(Attempting a measured tone.)
Of *course* I "*realized*" there was a sixty-five-year-old woman fighting *cancer* in here—I just also "*realized*" that she was *sleeping,* as she has been all *day,* as my mother has been *too,* because they're on a shit-load of *painkillers* and they feel like fucking *shit* because they have fucking *cancer,* okay?
(Letting some emotion slip.)
And when you're *sleeping* all day that means that you can't *hear* what anyone else is *saying,* so I thought it wouldn't *hurt* anyone if I practiced

my new *bits* in here for my mom, okay? Because this is what we like *doing*, okay?

>*(Very impassioned.)*

THIS. IS WHAT WE LIKE! DOING!!!

>*(Represses a little sob.)*

When she's *awake . . .!*

>*A beat.* DON *looks perhaps a bit chastened. Then—*

DON
>*(Dripping with contempt.)*

Your new "bits"?

KARLA

Yes.

DON

What are you *talking* about. What are *"bits"?* I actually literally have / no idea what *bits* are.

KARLA

Oh my *god* are you *retarded?* "Bits" is a term we use in *comedy*—I'm a stand-up *comedian* / for christ's sake—

DON

I / don't care!

KARLA

—and I'm trying to generate some new *material* because I haven't had any new material in like six fucking *months*, so I'm like grasping at fucking *straws* here, okay, and I really don't need you like breathing down my *neck* and trying to like *edit* me—

DON

I'm / not trying to *edit* you, I just want you to SHUT. UP!

KARLA

—when what I'm doing actually has nothing to fucking *do* with you, I'm just trying to like be *creative* and get some *bonding* time in with my *mom!*

DON
>*(An explosion—still in a harsh whisper.)*

YOU CAN'T DO BOTH! You can't *both* be creative and get *"bonding time"* in with your mom! I mean, what else do you want to do—get an herbal colonic while you're at it?!

                    KARLA
What the fuck is wrong / *with you?!*

                    DON
        (Pulling out all the stops in a vicious cross-fire.)
NO, what the—F—is wrong with *YOU* and your self-obsessed hipster
ME GENERATION?! *Your mom is in the hospital with cancer.* Things
are *not looking good.* Things are looking, in fact, *pretty grim.*
        (Building to a whisper-scream.)
So *GIVE UP THE COMEDY FOR A HOT SECOND.* LET IT GO. PUT
IT ON THE BACK BURNER. Oh, and *here's* a radical idea: drop the
VIBRATOR JOKES and *FOCUS ON YOUR MOM!!!*

                    KARLA
        (Whisper-screaming, too.)
I *AM* FOCUSING ON MY MOM. And she fucking *LIKES* VIBRATOR
JOKES!!!

                    DON
        (Darkly sardonic.)
Yeah. Seems like they're really *killing* over there.
        KARLA*'s entire being seems to almost vibrate with white-*
        hot rage.

                    KARLA
You know what? You don't know anything *about* me OR my mom OR
her fucking cancer / or—

                    DON
No, I don't. / I don't know anything about your mom.

                    KARLA
No. You don't!

                    DON
You're right! I don't know your mom's *name.* I don't even know what
your mom / looks like.

                    KARLA
No, you don't. You don't! / You *don't.*

                    DON
She was just moved in to *my* mother's room this morning! How could
I know / anything about her?

KARLA

Exactly. / *Exactly.*

DON

(With saccharine-sweet irony.)

I don't even know what your mom's favorite *color* is, what her favorite *scent* is, what her favorite—

KARLA

Oh / you're an *asshole.*

DON

—National *Park* is, what her favorite *pet* name is, her favorite *sexual* / position . . .

KARLA

You're a fucking / *sociopath!*

DON

I don't know *any* of these things, and it doesn't matter—because I *still know your mom.* Do you know why? *Do you know why?*

KARLA

Go *DIE.*

DON

Because she's in the *gynecologic oncology unit.* And I know, now, that those things about your mom that "make her who she is"? Those things *don't matter anymore.*

DON*'s cell phone vibrates. He takes it out and silences it.*

DON

Because everything your mom is? Everything she likes? Everything she hates? Everything you love about her? Everything you hate? Everything she does that drives you crazy? Everything she says that gives you nightmares? Everything that you have spent the last ten years complaining about to your *shrink?*

His cell phone vibrates again—he takes it out and silences it, angrily.

DON

You will find yourself praying—*praying,* little *girl*—that she could do those things *one more time.* Because *all your mom is now is cancer.*

(He pants.)

That's it. That's all.

> *(He catches his breath.)*

You'll see. You'll see.

> *(Trying not to cry.)*

That's all she is now. You'll see.

> *A beat.* DON*'s cell phone vibrates again—he takes it out and silences it with ferocious fury. Then—*

KARLA

My mom's never been sick a day in her life. This was just . . . a fluke. And they caught it early. So.

DON

Uh-huh.

KARLA

And she had a hysterectomy. So.

DON

Uh-huh.

KARLA

I mean it was just Stage 1! Endometrial.

> *(Beat.)*

Papillary serous carcin*oma*. But still.

> *(Beat.)*

She's gonna be *fine*.

DON

Uh-huh.

KARLA

What do you *mean*, "UH-HUH"?

DON

Nothing.

> *(Beat.)*

Just. . . "uh-huh."

> *A beat.* KARLA *silently fumes. Then—*

> DON*'s cell phone vibrates again. He takes it out of his pocket, looks at it, reads something on it that makes him nearly homicidal, and shoves it back in his pocket. Gets up*

and pours himself a Dixie cup of water. Sips it, furiously.
Exhales, loudly.

Meanwhile, KARLA *takes her hair out of a ponytail. Shakes*
it out. Puts it back in a low ponytail. Takes a sip of water
from her Dixie cup. Looks at her mom. Then—furiously
scribbles in her notebook.

KARLA
(Unintelligible mutter.)

DON
I'm sorry?

KARLA
(Very softly, nearly unintelligible.)
. . . you're a fucking joke . . .

DON
(Truly didn't hear her.)
I'm *sorry?*

KARLA
You're a fucking *joke? YOU'RE A FUCKING JOKE?*

DON
Ah. Yes.
(Almost calmly—eerily so.)
I'm a "fucking joke." Got it. How interesting. How well put. Well let me
ask you this. Let me ask you *this*: if I am, indeed, as you say, a "fucking
joke," then let me ask you THIS:
And suddenly he whips over to the curtain and violently
draws it aside. KARLA *spins around, startled.*

DON
(Right in her face.)
DOES IT LOOK LIKE I'M LAUGHING? *DOES IT LOOK LIKE I'M—*
KARLA *throws her Dixie cup of water in* DON*'s face.*

KARLA
YOU DON'T EVEN KNOW HOW TO LAUGH.
And without skipping a beat, DON *throws his Dixie cup of*
water in KARLA*'s face. Then—*

Without skipping a beat, KARLA *pantses* DON —*grabs his sweatpants by the waist and yanks them, forcefully, down to his ankles.*

He stands there—his skinny, sickly-white legs exposed— wearing terribly unflattering, billowy Tweety-Bird-patterned boxers.

A beat. Their eyes are locked. They are frozen, breathing heavily, alive. Then—

KARLA

Okay, I don't even know what to say about those boxers? So I'm gonna start with the sweatpants.

(Takes them in.)

Those sweatpants are a hate crime.

DON *doesn't respond.*

KARLA

What kind of a self-respecting middle-aged man wears fucking *sweatpants.*

He is utterly still. Says nothing.

KARLA

What kind of a narcissistic piece of *shit* wears a pair of *Tweety Bird boxers* under his fucking *sweatpants* to a *hospital* where his mother is DYING.

KARLA *immediately looks a tinge contrite—but covers it well; maintains eye contact with* DON, *unflinching.*

DON *blinks—then finally bends down and pulls up his sweatpants.*

DON

(Matter-of-fact.)

When your mother's been dying for seven years, you sort of stop noticing what kind of boxers you're wearing, okay?

He draws the curtain back. Sits in his chair. Rubs his temples. Hangs his head in his hands.

KARLA *chews a cuticle. Starts to say something. Stops herself. A beat. Then—*

KARLA

That still doesn't explain the sweatpants.

DON *can't believe she's still going.*

>   KARLA

Nothing explains those.

> *His face turns red—he looks utterly irate, like he really might explode. Then—*
>
> *He looks down at his sweatpants . . . and starts to laugh.*
>
> KARLA *listens. A beat. Then—*

>   KARLA

Are you . . .

>   DON

You're right.

> *(Giggles uncontrollably.)*

They're so . . . *ugly* . . .!

>   KARLA

They're not that bad. . . .

>   DON

> *(Deeply examining his sweatpants.)*

They're seriously the ugliest things I've ever *seen!*

> KARLA *starts to laugh, now, too.*

>   KARLA

I know I was just saying that to make you feel better they're *so* ugly.

> DON *examines his pants closely.*

>   DON

> *(Giggling like a little boy.)*

Why did I . . . *buy* . . . these things . . .?!

>   KARLA

I don't know!

>   DON

What was I *thinking?!*

>   KARLA

I think you weren't!

>   DON

> *(Giggling hysterically.)*

I think I wasn't . . .!

> *(Giggling wanes.)*

I think I wasn't.

> *(Suddenly stops giggling.)*

I think I wasn't thinking.

> DON *sits in his chair, heavily—like a bag of bricks hitting the ground.*

DON

> *(A huge, disastrous revelation.)*

Oh . . . god. I wasn't . . . thinking.

> *Suddenly, his face turns kind of pink, and kind of crinkles, again. And then . . .*
>
> *He starts to cry. He tries very hard not to let* KARLA *hear.*

KARLA

> *(Delicately.)*

Are you—

DON

No!

KARLA

You don't even know what I was gonna ask . . .

DON

> *(Wiping nose on sleeve.)*

Yes I do—I'm not an *idiot.*

KARLA

I was gonna ask . . . are you . . .

> *(Fishing.)*

. . . a Sagittarius? Because you seem like a Sagittarius.

DON

No you weren't.

KARLA

I was gonna ask are you . . . gonna finish those fries? 'Cause they look really good!

DON

> *(Laughing a bit, in spite of himself.)*

I'm not even *eating* fries . . .!

KARLA
(Happy she made him laugh.)
I was gonna ask are you . . . afraid of heights?

DON
No.

KARLA
Are you superstitious?

DON
No.

KARLA
Are you a sweet or savory kind of person?

DON
Savory.

KARLA
Are you a Yankees or Mets fan?

DON
(A ridiculous question.)
METS!

KARLA
Jeez, okay. Are you a dog or cat person?

DON
(Another ridiculous question.)
DOG!

KARLA
Are you a Democrat?

DON
Yes.

KARLA
Are you a homeowner?

DON
Yes.

KARLA
Are you in love?
A beat. Then—

He emits a fantastically loud sob. And then another. He sobs.
Can't control it. Stops trying to hide the fact that he's crying.
Lets go of any attempt at manliness or dignity-retention,
and sobs. Like a baby. Like the bereaved.

KARLA

Oh no. Oh no . . .! I'm sorry—I'm—

DON

My wife left me three months ago . . .!
(Sobs)
I don't know what to do . . .!
(Weeps.)
I don't know who I *am*, anymore . . .!
(Wails.)
I have *nothing!*

He sobs hysterically. It gets pretty loud. KARLA *looks to see*
if MARCIE *has been woken. She still sleeps.*

DON *sobs. Pulls at his hair.*

DON

I have NOTHING!!!

He sobs a beat more. Then—

He tires out from sobbing. Stops pulling his hair. Wipes his
nose on his sleeve. Looks at the space in front of him—
his eyes glassy, his mind somewhere else. Then—

He looks at his mother, lying dead to the world in her
hospital bed—her face still puckered fiercely like a sour
lemon. He reaches for GEENA's *hand; takes her limp fingers*
in his, gives them a squeeze.

DON

(Tiny, dead voice.)
I have nothing.

He hangs his head in his hands. He looks like a portrait of
misery.

A beat. Then—

Very slowly, and very softly, KARLA *approaches the curtain*
and draws it aside. She looks at DON. *His head still hangs*
in his hands.

KARLA

Hey.

He looks up, surprised to see her there.

DON

Hey . . .

(Beat.)

KARLA

I'm sorry.

(Beat.)

DON

I'm sorry.

(Beat.)

I mean it this time.

KARLA *takes a step toward him, and extends her hand.*

KARLA

I'm Karla.

DON *stands, and extends his hand.*

DON

Don.

They shake hands.

DON

Wow . . .

KARLA

What?

DON

You have a really . . . *firm* /. . . handshake . . .

KARLA

Oh, I know—it's something my mom always, like, *drilled* into us when we were kids.

DON

Really?

KARLA

Yeah, she would always be like: "A weak handshake is an invitation for someone to fuck you over."

DON

Whoa.

KARLA

I know.

DON

I mean, I think I *agree* with her, / but . . .

KARLA

I / know.

DON

I've just never heard it *phrased* quite that way.

KARLA

I know. She has a . . . well. Let's just say that some of her parenting methods? Have been . . . unorthodox.

DON

(Shrugs.)

My mom used to bring me to her book club and point at the hors d'oeuvres and say: "Eat up, 'cause that's your dinner!"

KARLA

If my sister and I refused to eat dinner? My mom would march into the other room and start packing a suitcase.

DON

My mom used to put me to sleep by telling me stories about all the men she'd pursued romantically before my dad.

KARLA

My mom used to put us to sleep by turning on "SV Squad."

DON

You mean the show that's all about sex crimes?

KARLA

(Grinning, nodding.)

YUP.

DON

That's how she put you to sleep?

KARLA

We found it soothing!

DON
You find "SV Squad" soothing?!

KARLA
Well, now we've graduated to "SV Ped," but—

DON
What is "SV Ped"?!

KARLA
It specifically examines child-related sex crimes?

DON
Jesus . . . / christ.

KARLA
It's a way better show. The performances are subtler. The writing is exemplary. The kids are really cute—until they get kidnapped and—

DON
Just stop.

KARLA
'K sorry.

DON
(Can't wrap head aroung this.)
So now you fall asleep to "SV *Ped*"?!

KARLA
My mom does, like, every night. And I do sometimes.

DON
What about your sister?
Something shifts in KARLA. *Her face falls, a bit. She becomes darker.*

KARLA
Um. . . .
(Beat.)
No, she doesn't.
(Beat.)

DON
Oh.

Suddenly, from the other side of the room:

MARCIE

(A hoarse croak.)
She's dead.

DON *and* KARLA *look immediately at* MARCIE, *who appears to be still asleep. A beat. Then —*

KARLA *bursts out laughing.*

KARLA

(Laughing uncontrollably.)
I'm sorry — I'm sorry . . .!
(Can't stop laughing.)
I'm not laughing 'cause she's dead — 'cause she definitely *is* dead, and that's definitely not funny, but that was just . . .
(Struggling to talk through laughing.)
. . . such good *timing* . . .!

DON *looks over at* MARCIE.

DON

Is she . . . still *asleep* . . .?
KARLA *looks too.*

KARLA

I think so . . .!
DON *starts to laugh, now, too.*

DON

That was so *weird* . . .!

KARLA

I know, right?!
(Imitating the croak.)
"She's dead."
They laugh.

DON

(Going even further with the croak-y imitation.)
"Sheee's deeead."
This cracks KARLA *up. They take it even further.*

KARLA	DON
(Really going for it.)	*(Really going for it.)*
"Sheeeeeeeeeeee's	"Sheeeeeeeeeeee's
deeeeeeeeeeeeaaaad!!!"	deeeeeeeeeeeeaaaad!!!"

*They both totally crack up. A long beat of just laughing.
Then—*

DON

That was a good "bit" . . .!
    (Beat.)

KARLA

Yeah, it was.

    KARLA *looks at* DON *and smiles. Her smile is full of sadness
and gratitude, heartbreak and hope.*

KARLA

It was a good bit. It was.

    DON *smiles at her, too.*

SCENE 2

A few days later.

KARLA *and* DON *sit in their respective visitors' chairs. They each have a styrofoam coffee cup near them, from the hospital cafeteria.*

They have pulled the plastic curtain aside so that they can now see each other. GEENA *and* MARCIE *lie in their beds, sleeping.*

Today DON *is wearing khakis which are not terribly flattering but which are definitely a vast improvement over the sweatpants. He wears nondescript sneakers and a worn tee-shirt. He still wears that very sad corduroy jacket. He has his feet up on the frame of his mother's hospital bed and reads from* The New Yorker.

KARLA *wears skinny jeans and sneakers and a different colorful ironic sweater. She scribbles in her notebook.*

Even though they are both in their own separate worlds, it is clear that DON *and* KARLA *have developed a casual sort of ease in their dynamic—in this unusual situation in which they find themselves.*

DON *laughs as he reads something funny in his magazine.*

DON

Heh.

DON

Ha. Ha!

(Beat.)

Heh heh heh heh heh . . .

He continues reading. It gets funnier. He tries to keep quiet so as not to wake the two sleeping women, but it's hard.

DON

Hahaha! Hahahahahahahahaha!

On the other side of the room, KARLA *is becoming increasingly incredulous. Finally—*

KARLA

What's so funny?

DON

Oh. Sorry. I. I didn't mean to ah. Laugh. So loud. I'll keep it down. Sorry.

KARLA

But what are you laughing at?

DON

You really wanna know?

KARLA

Yeah . . .

DON

Oh. I thought you were—I thought you were just saying "what's so funny" as a, um. As one of your euphemisms, and what you really meant was . . . "shut up."

(Beat.)

KARLA

(Slightly bemused.)
"One of my euphemisms"?

DON

You know, how you'll say stuff like: "Hey Don, I'm gonna go get some coffee from the cafeteria, do you want anything?" When what you really mean is: "Hey Don, can you go get me some coffee from the cafeteria?"

KARLA *laughs.* DON *smiles.*

DON

Or how you'll be like: "Hey Don, what time is it?" When what you really mean is: "Hey Don, it's time for you to go get me some coffee from the cafeteria."

KARLA *laughs, louder.* DON *smiles, wider.*

DON

Or how you'll be like: "Hey Don, it's nice to see you again," when what you really mean is: "Why are you still *here*, Don? When is this whole thing going to be *over* so I never have to see your face again?"

Beat. Deadly silence. It gets superawkward. Then—

Embarrassed, DON *returns to reading* The New Yorker.

KARLA

So *what's so funny?*

A beat. DON *hesitates. Takes his feet off the bed. Looks around. Makes sure* MARCIE *and* GEENA *are asleep. Then—*

DON

It's this, ah. I'm just rereading this, um. It's this . . . "Shouts & Murmurs" piece? In the . . . New Yorker? It's about. . . .

(He considers.)

Ahm. It's not a very . . . appropriate. . . .

(Beat.)

I'm not sure I should—it's sort of, um . . .

(Choosing words carefully.)

. . . *blue* . . . humor . . .?

(Beat.)

KARLA

Are you fucking kidding me, Don.

(Beat.)

DON

Okay it's about, um. It's about the life of a, uh. Of a . . . condom?

(Feels humiliated, but continues.)

It's. Ahmmm . . . It's from the point of view of a condom, but it's funny because you don't know?

(Beat.)

That it's a . . . condom . . .? At first you can't tell? What it . . .is?

(Beat.)

That's why it's . . . so funny?

He hopes he can just finish the conversation here. She doesn't give him anything.

A beat. Then—he continues, with great reluctance.

DON

So you don't know that it's a condom, you just . . . you know it, um, it lives in a wallet? And sometimes it gets taken *out* but um. Never . . . used? And it gets to, um, it gets to meet . . . all the other . . . things? That um, live? In the wallet, too?

A beat. KARLA *just stares at* DON. *He stares back at her.*
Then—he continues.

KARLA

Like, it meets its owner's NYU ID card, and um his library card and his
Jamba Juice card? (That part is really funny.) And eventually you, um. You
figure out that it's a . . . condom. You know? And that part is *really* funny.

It's all getting even more uncomfortable. He keeps going.

DON

So then later on in the piece, the owner of the, um, the wallet and the,
um, the *condom*, he um. He meets a girl? And he takes out the condom.
To, uh. You know . . .

(Beat.)

But—it's expired! He can't use it!

DON *laughs.* KARLA *does not.* DON *stops laughing. Continues.*

DON

But the girl he's with, ah. *She* has a condom. But the condom—*our*
condom (I mean I don't mean *our condom*, I mean—um, you know *the*
condom)—*that* condom gets . . . put into a box? And um.

(Gets a little misty-eyed.)

That box becomes like a . . . memory box? For the condom's owner?
And this new girl? For their *relationship*, I mean. So the condom now
gets to, ah, *meet* all these love notes and, um, movie stubs and various
sweet nothings et cetera that get put into the memory box? To com-
memorate the relationship? That started, ah, with the . . .

(Almost wistfully.)

. . . expired condom?

A beat. KARLA *stares at* DON. *He looks back at her. Then—*

KARLA

That doesn't sound funny *at all.*

DON

(A bit defensively.)

I think it is . . .

KARLA

My jokes are way better than that.

DON

You haven't even *read* it / yet.

44

KARLA

(Slouching down in her chair.)

My jokes are better than everyone's.

KARLA *sulks.* DON *goes back to his magazine.*

A beat. Then—

MARLA

I just.

(Beat.)

I . . . have a hard time with—with other . . . comedy. Writers.

DON

Oh.

KARLA

It's like—I cannot let anyone have *any* amount of success at what I love doing, who isn't me.

DON

Okay.

KARLA

It's like—it's like, *I* want to be the *only* successful comedian. In the *world.*

(Beat.)

I'm insane.

(Really thinks about it,)

I'm *insane. . . .*

(Beat.)

DON

You're not insane.

KARLA

I'm insane.

DON

I mean, I used to feel that way? All the time.

(Beat.)

KARLA

Really?

DON

Oh my *god*, yeah. I couldn't *stand* anyone being even re*motely* more successful than me at what I wanted to do.

KARLA

What did you want to do?

DON

(Suddenly embarrassed.)
Just . . . y'know. What I do. For a . . . living. . . .

KARLA

Which is what? I don't actually really know / you, Don.

DON

Oh. Um. It doesn't matter. Just um. Tech. Stuff?

KARLA

So you're like an IT guy?

DON

Oh. I guess I was. I don't know. I guess I was . . . I'm not. Anymore.

KARLA

So what are you *now?*

DON

I'm . . . nothing.
(Beat.)

KARLA

That's depressing.

DON

No! I mean I—I *sold* my startup. I sold it for . . . I sold it a few years ago.

KARLA

You sold it for . . .?

DON

What?

KARLA

What did you sell it for?

DON

(Very uncomfortable.)
Oh. Um.
(Beat.)
Money . . .?
(Beat.)

MARLA

(Putting it together.)

Wait. You sold your tech startup for . . . so much money that now . . . you can do *nothing?*

DON

(Shrugs.)

I guess.

> KARLA*'s shakes her head, as if the act of shaking her brain will help her wrap her mind around what she is now learning about* DON.

KARLA

Whoa. Whoa! So you're . . . like a . . . *millionaire* . . .

DON

(Mortified.)

It doesn't really matter.

KARLA

But you look like a *homeless person.*

DON

Oh, thanks.

KARLA

Your shoes have holes in them . . .!

DON

(Looks at his shoes, suddenly self-conscious.)

They do?

KARLA

Your sad little corduroy jacket doesn't have *elbows.*

DON

Hey, it's been a rough couple of months!

> *A beat.* DON *looks away.* KARLA *chews a cuticle. Looks at* DON, *contemplatively. Then—*

KARLA

I like you *soooooo* much better now that I know you're a millionaire.

DON

(Sadly.)

A lotta people do.

(Beat.)

47

KARLA

Is your apartment really nice?

DON

What?

KARLA

I have a bunch of questions that I always wanna ask rich people?
But I never do because it's rude, of course?

DON

Okay.

KARLA

Where do you live?
    (Beat.)

DON

    (Reluctantly.)
Central Park West?

KARLA

In like one of those huge doorman buildings?

DON

Uh. Yeah?

KARLA

How many bedrooms?

DON

Why do you care? Five.

KARLA

FIVE?!

DON

One of them we use as an office.

KARLA

For what?! You don't even *work!*

DON

Well, you know, I / still need—

KARLA

Did you have an interior decorator *design* it?

DON

You have a lot of issues around money.

KARLA

No I don't, shut up. What's the color palette?

DON

What? I don't know. Sea foam green?

KARLA

"Sea foam green"?

DON

(With some embarrassment.)

Yeah. . . .

KARLA

I don't understand.

DON

What do you mean / you don't—

KARLA

You mean the *accents* are "sea foam green"?

DON

No, the—

KARLA

The entire *apartment* is "sea foam green"?!

DON

Yeah, the—

KARLA

Wait, so you have like a "sea foam green" couch and like a "sea foam green" rug and like the *walls* are "sea foam green"? And the *lighting* fixtures are—

DON

(Suddenly erupting.)

I don't *know*, okay?! I DON'T REMEMBER.

A beat. Then—

KARLA

I'm sorry.

(Beat.)

49

DON

I'm sorry. I just.

    (Beat.)

I haven't been there . . . in. A couple of months.

    (Beat.)

I'm . . . subletting. A place. A few blocks away from my old . . .

    (Beat.)

I don't know why I decided to stay in the same neighborhood. Stupid. I guess I thought it would be easier. For . . .

    (Beat.)

Anyway. It's *not*. So.

    (Beat.)

And I *hate* my new place. Nothing in it is *mine*. And.

    (Beat.)

I don't know. Maybe it's not so bad.

    (Beat.)

KARLA

Well I bet your new place that you hate? Is like ten *thousand* times nicer than my apartment.

    DON *laughs.* KARLA *smiles.*

DON

Money doesn't change your life as much as you think it will.

KARLA

That's just something rich people say to make poor people feel better.

DON

It doesn't! So you can, what. Buy a nice car? Get a flatscreen TV? Take a cool *vacation*? Those things don't fix . . .

    (Indicates his head, vaguely.)

. . . you know. What's in *here*, . . .

KARLA

    (Teasing him.)

What's . . . *in* . . . there . . .?

DON

    (Frustrated, now.)

Never mind.

KARLA

Okay.

DON

Never *mind.*
(*Beat.*)

KARLA

(*Trying to soften the moment.*)
Yeah, and you probably don't even buy yourself new TVs or vacations
or cars or anything, I bet.

DON

What do you—

KARLA

You won't even buy me a cup of coffee!

DON

I get you coffee all the time!

KARLA

Yeah but you always make me pay you *back.*

DON

Well, it—

KARLA

And you always *text* me the *exact* amount that I *owe* you. Like, *while*
you're buying it.

DON

Well, it's—

KARLA

You're always like, "Hi Karla. Your almond milk latte was $5.23. Exact
change would be preferable, please."

DON

Well it is very overpriced, here!
A beat. She smiles. He softens. Then—

KARLA

But the money does help with . . .
(*Indicates the hospital room.*)
This.

He just looks at her.

KARLA

I mean you don't have to worry about *any* of this shit, right? Like, you don't even *need* insurance.

DON

(Very uncomfortable.)

I don't know.

KARLA

Wow.

(Puts her feet up on her mother's hospital bed.)

Wow.

(Beat.)

DON

Does your mother—

KARLA

Oh, her insurance is *terrible.* Which is hilarious, 'cause she's a social worker. It's like, "Thanks for the help, U.S. Government!"

(Chuckles.)

We're totally fucked.

(Laughs.)

I should probably just kill myself.

She laughs. A beat. DON *regards* KARLA, *with concern.*

KARLA

That was a joke. I'm not going to kill myself.

(Beat.)

Today.

A beat. DON *continues to regard* KARLA *with yet more concern.*

KARLA

That was a *joke!* God. You do not understand my charming and irreverent dark sense of humor at *all.*

A beat. She returns to her notebook. Scribbles a little. He continues to take her in. Then—

DON

What do you *mean* you're . . . "fucked"?

KARLA

Just that—I mean, we're not *fucked*, I was being dramatic. We're just—it's just. . . .

(*Beat.*)

I mean, her insurance is great in a lot of ways—they paid for her surgery and her week of recovery here which is awesome, but then when it comes to, like, the chemo and the radiation and the medications, it's just . . . It's gonna be tougher.

(*Beat.*)

But don't worry, Don. You looked so *worried* right now. It's *fine*. This is how the world *works*. Shit happens, and you just—you figure it out. Or . . . you don't. You just accept that life is . . . kind of shitty. And that's okay. And maybe it'll change. Or maybe it won't. And that's okay too! Or maybe it's not. And maybe it's okay that it's not okay. You know?

DON *regards* KARLA, *seriously.*

KARLA

No, of course you don't. You have like seven gajillion *dollars*, so if your mom dies, you can just, like . . . buy a new one.

DON *does not laugh.*

KARLA

Sorry. That was another attempt at a dark joke and it . . . yeah it wasn't the time. I acknowledge that. Sorry.

DON

I—

KARLA

Timing is everything.

DON

Okay. I—

KARLA

(*In an old time-y vaudevillian voice*)
"What is the secret to great comedy?"

DON

Um. I don't know. What is the—

KARLA

TIMING!

A beat. He does not laugh. Then—

DON
(With deep concern for her.)
Karla, I just—

KARLA
(Suddenly erupting.)
Don, would you stop?! You don't *know* me—you don't have to *worry* about me.
(Beat.)
It's really condescending, actually.
(Beat.)

DON
I'm sorry.

> *She takes her feet off the bed.*
>
> DON *tries to read his* New Yorker. *We can tell that he's not really reading at all. Just worrying and fretting.*
>
> KARLA *looks at her notebook, scribbles a bit. Several moments of quiet between them. Then—*

KARLA
What was your tech startup?

DON
What? / Oh.

KARLA
What was your—

DON
It was. Ahm. It was, um. PerfectWeddingMatches? Dot com . . .?
(Beat.)

KARLA
I'm *sorry*?

DON
Yeah.

KARLA
(Almost with disgust.)
What *is* that?

DON
It's / ahm, . . .

KARLA

It sounds *terrible.*

DON

You've never heard of it?

KARLA *just looks at him.*

KARLA

Okay. Just. A lot of women. Ah. It's a pretty *popular* . . . Um. Anyway.
(*Beat.*)
It's like, um. The site helps you find the perfect matches for all the services you would need for your perfect wedding? It's like a match-making service? But for wedding planning?

KARLA *stares blankly at* DON.

DON

So you and your partner answer a, um, seventy-nine-question person-ality quiz, designed by clinical psychologists to best elucidate your key personality *features*, and then based on what the algorithm devises from your *answers*, we set you up with the best options specially tailored *for you*, for your perfect wedding. Perfect venue, perfect invi-tations, perfect caterer, perfect porta-potties, perfect everything.
(*Desperately trying to be cheerful.*)
And, at the same time, you get to learn more about your partner. So, really, it's a win-win . . .!
(*Willing himself to stay positive.*)
It's actually helped a lot of people.
(*Fighting despair.*)
Over five million users.

KARLA *looks at* DON, *utterly bewildered.*

KARLA

How did you even come *up* with that?

DON

It was my wife's idea.

KARLA

Do you even *give* a shit about weddings?

DON

(*A sad chuckle.*)
Couldn't care less!

KARLA

Whoa. . . .

>(Processes the inherent. tragedy in DON's tale.)

So, you spent years / and years—

DON

Hey / watch it. . . .

KARLA

—your whole *youth*—building up this business with a woman who would eventually *leave* you—

DON

Okay / we don't have to get—

KARLA

—and the business was something you didn't even *give* a shit about?

DON

>(Sharply.)

Well, it was obviously a worthwhile investment!

>*A beat. Then*—DON *goes back to reading* The New Yorker. *Angrily, now.*

>KARLA *goes back to writing in her notebook. Then*—

>DON's *cell phone vibrates.*

DON

Oh jesus chr—

>*He takes the phone out of his pocket, unlocks it and reads something on it.*

>*As he reads, the blood begins to drain from his face. His jaw tightens. His eyes glass over.*

>KARLA *looks at him, with growing concern. Then*—

>DON *puts his cell phone down and treads over to the bathroom. Steps inside and gingerly shuts the door. Then*—

>*We hear a series of piercing screams, accompanied by mournful wails and intense wall-banging from inside the bathroom.*

>KARLA *looks at the bathroom door, horrified. After a moment, the noises stop. Then*—

DON *emerges from the bathroom, utterly calm—as if nothing just happened. He returns to his chair. After a beat:*

KARLA

What?
(Beat.)

DON

It was a text. From . . . my son.

KARLA

I didn't even / know you—

DON

I try not to talk about him because he makes me so . . .
(Beat.)

KARLA

(Delicately.)
Well . . . what did he say?
DON *looks like he might cry.*

KARLA

You don't have to—

DON

No, it's okay.
(Picks up the phone.)
He wrote:
(Reads from phone.)
"Hey Dad hope you are having a good Sunday with Grandma. I just wanted you to know I took out three thousand dollars from your bank account. I know you changed the pin but you're a fucking idiot and I found out what the new pin is because you e-mailed it to Mom and I hacked into her e-mail ha ha haha ha you're so dumb that you didn't even think I would know how to do that. Maybe if you had responded to any of my fucking texts like an attentive fucking parent I wouldn't have had to do this but since you always fucking ignore me I guess I had no choice. I am sorry if this is upsetting to you but at least I am being honest. Peace, Malcolm."
(Beat.)

KARLA

Whoa.

DON

I know.

KARLA

That's . . .

DON

I *know*.

KARLA

. . . a *long* . . . text. . . .

DON

What? Oh, I know. He always writes me these massively long texts. Which I find ironic, since he's actually spoken about *eighteen* words to me in the last two years. It would be delightful if he could be comparably loquacious and articulate in his high school *English* papers, but wait, he would have to have *not dropped out of high school* for that to be the case.

> *He picks up his cell phone and begins to type, ragefully.*

KARLA

What are you doing?

DON

Texting him back.

KARLA

Don't!

DON

Why?

KARLA

Because . . . you're angry. And—you might say something that you . . . can't take back.

> *A beat. Then—*DON *sullenly throws his phone back down on his mother's bed.*
>
> *He sits down in his chair. Rests his weary head in his hands.* KARLA *watches him. Then—*

KARLA

So . . . what the fuck is *wrong* with him?

DON

(Despondent.)

He's a teenager.

KARLA

Yeah, but like . . . that text was *intense*.

DON *shrugs.*

KARLA

Is he on *drugs?*

A beat. Then—DON *nods.*

KARLA

I *knew* it! I have like a sixth sense for that kind of stuff (not to brag). What kinds?

DON

(With some reluctance.)

Anything. Everything. Pills, mostly. He stole a ton of *her* pills, a few weeks ago.

(Indicates GEENA.*)*

I found out. That's why he doesn't come here anymore. That's why I don't respond to his stupid texts.

(Beat.)

That's why I'm all alone.

And my cunt ex-wife is too busy *finger* banging her new *girlfriend* to step up and, oh, I don't know, be a fucking *parent,* so—

KARLA

(Trying to calm him down.)

Okay, *okay*—

DON

I'm sorry.

KARLA

It's okay.

(Beat.)

I mean, it sounds like—I mean like, in all fairness, your life is like, *terrible,* right now.

DON *starts to laugh, a little. So does* KARLA. *Then*—

KARLA

He'll be okay, you know.

DON

(Sarcastically.)

That's really reassuring. Thanks.

KARLA

He will. He's just . . . going through a phase. A lot of kids go through that. Especially in New York City—oh my god. I did a *ton* of drugs in high school—we all did. I'm amazed I still even have a nose . . .!

DON

Ew.

KARLA

But then I just kinda . . . grew out of it.
    (Beat.)
And your son will, too.

    DON *lets this sink in. Makes a decision to actually try to be*
    hopeful for once in his life.

DON

How did you . . . grow out of it?

KARLA

Idunno . . . I guess I just sort of woke up one day? And was like, "How the fuck am I ever gonna be successful if I'm like partying until five in the morning every night and like routinely waking up next to some interchangeable overweight comedian whose jokes are like exclusively slanted towards *misogyny*, and the next thing I know I'm like *begging* him to let me give him a blowjob because of my ever-lingering *daddy* issues before I embark on the nightmarish walk of shame back to my tiny depressing apartment that I share with three strangers whom I *hate*, as I cry and chain-smoke cigarettes and talk out *loud* to myself while pretending I'm on the *phone*, and then just begin the whole cycle all over again that *night*?" You know?
    (Beat.)

DON

Uh. . . .

KARLA

And also I had kind of a wake-up call, I guess.

DON

What was your wake-up call?

KARLA

Oh. Um.
    (Beat.)
My sister died.

(Indicates MARCIE.*)*
As you heard.

KARLA

Right.

KARLA

"Sheee's deeea—"

KARLA

(Cutting her off.)
How did she die? If you don't mind / my—

KARLA

(Matter-of-fact.)
Oh yeah no it's fine—it was a drug overdose.
(Beat.)

DON

What?!

KARLA

(Oblivious.)
What?
(Suddenly realizing.)
Oh, shit—but—that doesn't mean that your *son* will die of a drug overdose! Y'know . . .
(Scrambling.)
. . . everyone's . . .
(Weakly.)
. . . different . . .

DON *hangs his head in his hands.* KARLA *stares at him, trying to conjure a way to reverse the effects of her blunder. Then—*

MARCIE

Who do I have to fuck around here to get a fizzy water.

KARLA *suddenly flinches—almost violently—at the sound of her mother's voice.* DON *notices.*

KARLA

One second, Mom. I'll go get it. One second.

KARLA *leaves and heads down the corridor.*

> DON *is left alone with the now-conscious* MARCIE, *whose*
> *eyes are still closed. He looks at her. Looks away. Stuffs*
> *his hands in his pockets. Pulls out some wadded-up tissues.*
> *Examines them. Throws them out in a trash bin by* GEENA's
> *bedstand. Then, thinks better of this and pulls a tissue out*
> *of the trash. Re-pockets it. He sits back down next to his*
> *mother. Picks up his* New Yorker. *Tries to read.*
>
> *A long moment. Then—*

MARCIE

You're not very social.

DON

Oh! Ahm. Are you, ah. Are you . . . talking. To me?

MARCIE

No, I'm talking to your comatose mother.

DON

Oh.

MARCIE

That was a joke.

DON

Okay.

MARCIE

Because she's always sleeping.

DON

Okay.

MARCIE

Because she has cancer.

DON

(*Terribly uncomfortable.*)
Okay.
(*Beat.*)

MARCIE

I can make cancer jokes. Because *I* have cancer.

DON

Okay.

MARCIE

Like how Jews can make Jewish jokes?

DON

Okay.

MARCIE

Are you Jewish?

DON

What?

MARCIE

You must be. You're funny.

DON

(Flattered.)

Oh . . .!

MARCIE

That was a joke. You're not funny.

DON

(Heartbroken.)

Oh.

(Beat.)

MARCIE

I used to be *married* to a Jew.

DON

Okay.

MARCIE

Thought that meant that I could make *Jewish* jokes.

DON

Okay.

MARCIE

Turns out? That was NOT the case.

DON

Okay.

MARCIE

So I'm really trying to milk the *cancer* jokes.

DON

Okay.

MARCIE

While I can.

MARCIE *lies with her eyes closed. She tries to breathe, but is having trouble.*

MARCIE

This oxygen tube feels like it's raping my nose.

DON

Oh. Um. Do you want me to—

MARCIE

What're you gonna do, enlarge my nostrils with your dick?

DON

Um.
   (Beat.)

DON

I could get you a new . . . nasal . . . cannula . . .?

MARCIE
   (Turning head to the wall.)
I'll make Karla ask the nurse to replace it.
   (Beat.)
About time she did *something* useful.

DON

Um.
   A long beat. Then—

MARCIE
   (Turning back to DON.*)*
Was that rape joke too much for you?

DON

What?

MARCIE

Some men are very uncomfortable with rape jokes.

DON

Well—

MARCIE

Not all. But some.

DON

Yeah, I—

MARCIE

Usually the ones who have been accused of *rape*.

> *A long beat.* MARCIE *lies there with her eyes closed.* DON *looks at anything other than* MARCIE. *Then—*

MARCIE

This is the first time you and I have been alone.

DON

> *(Nodding toward* GEENA.*)*

Well—

MARCIE

She doesn't count.

> *(Beat.)*

It's the first time we've really talked.

DON

I know. . . .

MARCIE

It's nice.

> *A beat.* MARCIE *looks at the wall.* DON *looks at the back of* MARCIE*'s head. Then—*

MARCIE

> *(Turning her head to* DON.*)*

I liked that condom story.

DON

You—you did . . .?

MARCIE

Of course. It was brilliant.

DON

I thought so, too!

MARCIE

Karla is so self-centered. She can't appreciate anything outside her own head.

DON

Um.

> *(Beat.)*

MARCIE

So how 'bout you?

DON

Me . . .?

MARCIE

Rape jokes? Yay or nay.

DON

Oh. Ahmmm. Well. They're not my . . . *favorite*? But um. I'm sort of, uh
. . . used to them? Now?
    (Beat.)
Because of, ah. Karla?
    (Beat.)
You know, her—

MARCIE

Karla doesn't make a lot of jokes with me.
    (Beat.)

DON

But—what do you think of her . . . *bits?*

MARCIE

    (Horrified.)
WHAT?

DON

    (Horrified as well.)
I mean! Her, um. Her . . . standup . . . routines . . .!

MARCIE

Idunno.
    (Beat.)
I went a few times. To see her perform. She didn't even buy me a drink.

DON

But . . . / she—

MARCIE

I work hard. I'm working with kids all day. Kids with real problems.
    (Beat.)
I'm a *social* worker. I'm actually doing something useful at my job. I'm
not getting paid fifteen bucks and a basket of *nachos* to get onstage
and ruminate about my twat six nights a week.
    (Beat.)

DON

Um—

MARCIE

So if I'm gonna go see a *comedy* show after a twelve-hour work day? *Helping kids?* I need.
(*Beat.*)
At least she could buy me a drink.
(*Beat.*)

DON

But doesn't she—

MARCIE

What.

DON

Doesn't Karla, um . . . practice? Her . . . standup routines? For you? She said that—

MARCIE

We don't spend a lotta time together.
KARLA *reenters with a Dixie cup of seltzer.*

KARLA

Here, Mom.
KARLA *approaches her mom with the cup.* MARCIE *does nothing.*

KARLA

Um.
KARLA *holds out the cup to her mom.* MARCIE *does nothing.*

MARCIE

I need someone to feed it to me.

KARLA

Oh. Okay.
KARLA *slowly and awkwardly brings the cup to* MARCIE*'s lips.*

MARCIE

(*Eyes still closed.*)
I want *him* to feed it to me.

KARLA

Oh.

MARCIE

I'm sick of you.

KARLA

Mom.

MARCIE

I'm kidding.

KARLA

Okay.

KARLA *brings the cup to* MARCIE*'s lips again.*

MARCIE

I do want him to feed it to me, though.

KARLA

(Stung.)

Oh.

(Beat.)

Why?

MARCIE

Because you bore me?

(Beat.)

MARCIE

What? Are you going to *cry?*

KARLA

No . . .

MARCIE

(To DON.)

When she was a little girl? *Everything* made her cry. "Time for dinner!"
She'd cry. "Take your plate to the sink!" Bawling. "Brush your teeth and
put your jammies on!" Hysterical sobs.

MARCIE *laughs, remembering.*

KARLA

Mom . . .

MARCIE

(A bark.)

What!

(To DON.*)*

She has a very *bleak* worldview. Always did. I'd say: "Go to bed" and
she'd hear: "Nobody loves you."

> KARLA
>
> *(Fighting tears.)*

Mom. . . .

> MARCIE

Don't argue with me I have cancer.

> KARLA *steps back. Looks away from her mom.*

> MARCIE
>
> *(Mockingly.)*

"Boo hoo hoo hoo hoo!"

> KARLA *says nothing. Tries very hard not to cry.* DON *watches
> her. Then—he gently approaches* KARLA *and takes the
> Dixie cup out of her hand. She lets him.*

> DON

Okay, um. Mrs. . . .

> MARCIE
>
> *(Demurely.)*

Call me Marcie.

> *He brings the cup to her lips.* KARLA *watches. He is very
> gentle.*

> DON

Okay, um, Marcie, I'm bringing the Dixie cup to your lips.

> MARCIE

Okay.

> DON

Okay now I'm just going to pour some seltzer into your mouth.

> MARCIE

Okay.

> DON

Can you open your mouth?

> MARCIE

Okay.

> MARCIE *opens her mouth, and* DON *delicately pours some
> seltzer from the Dixie cup into it.* KARLA *watches.* MARCIE
> *drinks.*

DON

Good job.

MARCIE *drinks the whole cup.*

MARCIE

I need more.

DON

Oh.

MARCIE

Get me more, Karla.

KARLA *says nothing. Takes the Dixie cup from* DON *and starts to leave.*

MARCIE
(Calling after KARLA.*)*

And can you tell the nurse I need a new nasal cannula while you're out there?

KARLA

Sure.

MARCIE

And a new daughter?

KARLA *stops. Then—she leaves.*

MARCIE *closes her eyes.* DON *looks at her, lost. And then—*

Silence.

MARCIE *lies there with her eyes closed.* DON *cannot tell if she's sleeping. He stands awkwardly next to her bed, looking at the back of her head, then around the room. Shoves his hands in his pockets. Takes them out. Looks at the wall.*

The moment feels like it goes on forever. And then—

DON

Why do you—

With a surprising and immediate burst of energy, MARCIE *suddenly makes a hammy, comical "dead" face—tongue lolling, eyes bugging out.*

MARCIE

Blehhhggghhh!!!

A beat. Then—

DON

What?

MARCIE

(Casually.)
Just practicing dying.

KARLA *enters, holding two Dixie cups.*

KARLA

I got two more cups.

MARCIE

Do you want an award.

KARLA *is silent. Hands a cup to* DON.

DON

Okay, Marcie? I'm going to feed you the second cup of seltzer, okay?

MARCIE *nods, eyes still closed.*

DON

Okay. I'm bringing the second cup up to your lips.
(He does so.)
Okay, I'm going to pour the—

MARCIE

I'm sorry, why are you *narrating* this?

DON

What?

MARCIE

Why are you *telling* me everything you're doing?

DON

Oh. Because . . . I guess because your eyes are closed?

MARCIE

Okay . . .

DON

And also, because. . .

MARCIE

What.

DON

It's—I think it's—this is going to sound so *strange* . . .

MARCIE

What.

DON

It's . . . my son? When he was . . . oh god, it's such a long story.

MARCIE

(Eyes still closed.)
Tell me.

KARLA

Tell us. . . .

MARCIE

(To KARLA.*)*
Shhhh!

KARLA *shrinks.* DON *notices. He continues with his story.*

DON

Okay. Well, when we—

MARCIE

Feed me seltzer while you tell me.

DON

Okay.

He brings the cup to MARCIE*'s lips and pours the seltzer into her mouth. She swallows.*

DON

Good.

She finishes drinking.

DON

(Placing Dixie cup in trash.)
Good job.

MARCIE

(Coquettishly.)
Thank you Don.

DON *smiles uncomfortably, sits in* KARLA*'s chair and continues his story.*

DON

Okay, so, my son? Um. His mom and I had been . . .

He clearly feels uncomfortable telling the story, but continues.

DON

Ah . . . *really* . . . wanting a kid, and, ahm. We couldn't. She couldn't. . . .
    (Beat.)
I'm sorry, this is—I don't need to get into all—

MARCIE

Keep telling the story.

DON

I don't know.

KARLA

Keep telling it!

MARCIE

    (Snapping at KARLA.*)*
I just *said* that.

    KARLA *shrinks again.* DON *notices. He takes a deep breath; continues.*

DON

So we, ah, when we found out that the, uh, the . . . *adoption* . . . had come through . . . we, ah. We were so . . . *excited* that we, ah, we started to read, um, every book on parenting that we could *find*. I mean, we were buying a new book pretty much every week . . .!
    (Remembers.)
And we would stay up late, *every night*, and read these books to each other . . .
    (Drifts into the memory.)
She would lay her head on my stomach . . . and I would read. . . .
    (Drifts; smiles, a bit.)
Or I would lay my head on her stomach . . . and she would read. And we'd pretend there was a baby in there. . . .
    (Drifts.)
And before we know it, it's the week before we're supposed to go get our son, and we are . . . just . . . *flipping out*, because we realize of course that we actually have *no idea* what to do . . .! I mean, all these books contradict each other—one book says: "Always do this one thing if you want your child to turn out to be not a serial killer," and another book says: "NEVER do this one thing if you want your child to turn out to be *not* a serial killer"—and it's the same thing!
    (Laughs, a little.)

And everyone tells you, of course, that once you *have* the baby, that your instinct just sort of, um, kicks in. But . . . we're adopting, right? So what if we, you know. What if our instinct, just . . . isn't there?

(Laughs, with some anxiety.)

And my wife is—you know, I'm getting kind of worried about her, actually. She's started pulling her hair out again, and she's lost all this weight, and I look at her one night, and she's standing over the kitchen sink and I realize that she's been washing the same dish for about twenty *minutes*, and I can feel my brain sort of start to want to explode . . .

(Remembers.)

But then, as I'm looking at her . . . a . . . calm . . . comes over me, suddenly. And I say to her: "Honey? *Honey.* Put down the dish. Come with me." And I bring her into the living room, and we laid down on the couch, and I laid my head on her stomach, and I said to her: "*All we can do now is wait.* And read. Let's just read *this one book.*"

(Remembers.)

"Let's pretend this is the only book in the world. . . ."

(Remembers.)

And we opened this new book. And it was written by these two Hungarian women—from Budapest, I think—and right away we could tell that it was so . . . *different* . . . from all the other stuff we had read. Because they wrote about—about *respecting* your child . . . And part of that respect, is, um . . .

(Becoming emotional.)

. . . is . . . is not treating them like they're just a dumb *baby*, you know? Not just wiping their face when you think it's too dirty, not just shoving food into their mouth when you think they're hungry. Not, you know, not —*condescending* to them . . . But instead, just . . . *telling* them what you're doing—*telling* your child:

(He begins to cry.)

"I'm going to wipe your face now, because you have chocolate on it. It's going to be uncomfortable, at first, because the wash cloth is going to be wet. But it's good for you. Here we go."

(He cries.)

"I'm putting you in the bath. It's going to be warm. It might also be a bit startling, at first. But it will become pleasant, soon. Be patient. Trust me."

(He cries, harder.)

"I'm putting you in your crib. It's time to go to sleep. Sleep can be scary, because you have to be alone with your thoughts. But you're going to be okay. You are not alone. Mommy and I are right here with you. We love you so much.

(He sobs.)

We love you . . .!

(He calms down a bit.)

Goodnight."

(He stops crying; a beat.)

And stuff like that.

> He wipes his eyes, his nose with his sleeve. He looks at MARCIE.

DON

Do you want the other cup? Of seltzer? Marcie . . .?

> MARCIE *snores. She has fallen back asleep.* DON *turns to* KARLA.

DON

(Amused.)

She's asleep . . .!

> KARLA *turns away.*

DON

Karla?

> KARLA *wipes her eyes with her hands, quickly.*

KARLA

What.

DON

Nothing.

(Beat.)

DON

Your mom. . . .

KARLA

What?!

DON

Nothing.

> She walks over to GEENA's side of the room and sits in DON's chair. She hangs her head in her hands, and cries.

DON *watches. Then—*

> KARLA
>
> *(Softly.)*

Sometimes I wish that she would just *die*.

> *(Beat.)*

> DON

I know.

> KARLA

I don't really mean that.

> *(Beat.)*

> DON

I know.

> KARLA
>
> *(Crying.)*

I don't know how . . . to do . . . this . . .!

> *(Beat.)*

> DON

I know.

> *A beat.* KARLA *cries. Then—*

> KARLA

You're such a good . . . *dad* . . .

> DON

Not really.

> KARLA
>
> *(Through tears.)*

You love your kid . . . so *much* . . . Even though he's so . . . fucked *up*.

> DON
>
> *(Laughs, a bit.)*

That's true . . .! It's true.

> DON *approaches* KARLA, *gently. She continues to cry. Both* GEENA *and* MARCIE *continue to sleep.* DON *kneels down in front of* KARLA *and delicately places a hand on her knee. She lets him.*

KARLA

(Weeping.)
She's so . . . *mean* . . . to me.

(Sobs.)
But I love her . . . so . . .

(Can barely get the word out.)
. . . *much.* . . .*!*

> KARLA *cries and cries, her face in her hands.* DON *rubs her knee.*

DON

I know. I know. . . .

> KARLA *cries. Then—*

> *She calms down. Breathes deeply. Stops sobbing. Lifts her face from her hands. Looks up. Looks at* DON. *He looks at her, too.*

> *Their eyes are locked. They are frozen, breathing heavily, alive. A beat. Then—*

> KARLA *suddenly grabs* DON*'s face and kisses him, hard.*

> DON *is shocked, at first, but then . . . he kisses her back. It is chaste, sweet—like two children who have escaped from their parents' watchful eyes to steal a first kiss in a secret hiding place. Then—*

> *It becomes intense. Passionate. Hot, even. They devour each other with their mouths.* KARLA *comes down off the chair and straddles* DON *on the floor.*

> DON *embraces this action fully—wraps his arms around her torso and pulls her closer to him. They inhale each other with their kissing.* DON *stands up, hoisting* KARLA *up with him. They continue to consume each other.* DON *begins to carry her toward the bathroom.*

> KARLA *breaks away from the kiss.*

KARLA

You're taking me to the handicap-accessible *bathroom?*

DON

(Suddenly sheepish.)
Uh . . . yeah? Is that terrible . . .?

KARLA

No. It's awesome.

She attacks his face with her mouth. He lets her; attacks hers back.

The rest of the conversation is had in between kisses—breathlessly, excitedly, in spurts. Also, in whispers, so they don't wake their mothers.

KARLA

(Sort of breathless.)

Wait one thing.

They kiss.

DON

(Sort of breathless, also.)

What.

They kiss.

KARLA

I'm not gonna have sex with you.

DON

Yeah. I mean, I assumed—

KARLA

What do you mean "you assumed"?

DON

Oh. I don't know. I just meant. Well, look at you.

KARLA

What?

DON

You're very attractive.

KARLA

Thanks.

She kisses him.

DON

And I'm—

KARLA

You're . . . what?

DON
I don't know. I haven't gone to the gym in, like, six years.

KARLA
Yeah but you're rich so I don't care.
She leans in to kiss him. He pulls away.

KARLA
That was a joke.

DON
Oh. Really?

KARLA
YES.
She kisses him. Hard. He kisses her back. A beat. Kissing. Then—

DON
I'm so sorry I have to put you down now.

KARLA
Okay.
He puts her down. Cracks his back. Then—they keep kissing.

DON
I like kissing you so much.
They keep kissing.

KARLA
Okay. Let's go.
KARLA pulls DON towards the bathroom. Before they get there, she stops.

KARLA
We can do like first and second base. But that's it.

DON
That sounds great.
They kiss.

KARLA
I need to set boundaries. Because I can get carried away.

DON

I get it.

> *They kiss. Then—*KARLA *pulls* DON *into the bathroom. The*
> *door stays open. They make out in there.*

KARLA

Also I should tell you that I've never really had a real relationship? So
this is all stuff I'm still really working on.

DON

Really?

KARLA

Please don't judge me.

DON

Sorry.

> *They kiss. Then—she steps away, maintaining cool eye*
> *contact with him as she slowly unbuttons and then unzips*
> *her pants. He looks at her, agog. Then—*
>
> *She hops up and into the sink. He lunges for her and they*
> *keep making out.*

KARLA

I didn't lose my virginity until I was, like, twenty-four? Because I had
just, like, *severe* abandonment and intimacy issues? I still struggle with
this, FYI.

> *He starts to take off her pants.*

KARLA

It's about my dad.

> *He starts to kiss her legs as he finishes removing her pants.*

KARLA

He left my mom when I was fourteen? He cheated on her with her best
friend, Candi. My mom never really recovered from it, I think.

> *He starts to pull off her underwear.*

DON

Is this okay?

KARLA

Uh-huh.

He removes her underwear, begins kissing her up her leg.

KARLA

And it was just really bad timing because my dad left at like the *exact age* that I started developing sexual feelings towards boys? And my dad was, like, the primary male in my life? And then he was just . . . *gone?*

He makes his way up to her inner thigh.

KARLA

And I would hear from him every couple of months, but like only in weird ways? Like he would send me a postcard written entirely in *crayon?* And I would be like, "Dad—

He starts to go down on her.

KARLA

(With a deep gasp of pleasure.)
—I'm *fourteen."*

He continues to go down on her. She continues to try to talk to him, but it's challenging, given the exquisite amount of pleasure she is experiencing.

KARLA

And it's weird, because it's not like he's *stupid—*I mean, he's a *History* professor, but . . .

(She moans.)

But anyway yeah so then for like *years*, whenever a man would try to get close to me? I'd assume that he was gonna abandon me. Because I believed I was inherently unlovable?

(She moans, louder.)

And then my sister died, so that was, like . . . *not* good for my abandonment issues. Ha ha.

(She groans with pleasure.)

I've been in a lot of therapy. In case you can't tell.

He keeps going down on her. It gets more intense. He pulls over a squatty potty from near the toilet, sits on it. Continues to go down on her.

She tries to keep talking despite her mounting pleasure.

KARLA

And so anyway yeah after I had sex for the first time I became just like this total slut? Because I thought that if I just fucked someone right away, he would, like, instantly fall in love with me?

(She moans, loudly.)

This did NOT work.

(She grunts, rabidly.)

And so basically I just became that girl that men wanted to fuck but, like, never make their girlfriend?

(She wails with pleasure.)

And so yeah now I'm just trying to, like . . . you know. . . *change* that . . .

She becomes suddenly emotional. A beat. Then—

DON

Wait, are you going to start crying again?

He reaches into his pocket and pulls out a tissue. Hands it up to her.

KARLA

(Tearful)

No. I don't know. Maybe. Yeah. But don't worry. I cry all the time. It means practically nothing.

She blows her nose with the tissue. He returns to going down on her. She moans, loudly, as she continues to blow her nose. Then—

KARLA

Wait.

(Takes his head in her hands.)

I have to ask you something.

DON

Okay.

KARLA

Did none of that scare you? What I just said?

DON

What? No.

KARLA

Really?

DON

Yeah, no. You seem pretty normal to me.

He returns to going down on her. She moans. Then—

KARLA

(Taking his head in her hands again.)
Really?

DON

Yeah. But maybe I'm just fucked up.

KARLA

You're definitely fucked up.

> *He continues going down on her. She moans. Moans. Then yelps, loudly.*

DON

Shhh . . .!

KARLA

Don't tell me to "shhh"!

DON

Sorry!

KARLA

Turn on the shower.

DON

What?!

KARLA

Turn on the shower! To make *noise.*

DON

Oh!

> DON *quickly pulls the bathroom door closed with his leg. Then—the sound of the running shower. Then . . .*

> *Stillness.* GEENA *and* MARCIE *sleep. We can hear soft, muffled noises of pleasure from the bathroom—coupled with the occasional beeps from the IV stands and the sound of the running shower.*

> *A long beat. Then—*

GEENA

This is weird.

(Beat.)

MARCIE

Totally.

(Beat.)

MARCIE

They're very selfish.

(Beat.)

GEENA

Who isn't.

MARCIE

Okay.

A beat. Then—

GEENA *starts to struggle with her breathing. She moans.*

In the bathroom, we hear louder moans from KARLA.

GEENA *moans.*

KARLA *moans.*

GEENA *moans, louder.*

In the bathroom, we hear KARLA *climaxing. Then—*

GEENA

(Reaching her hand toward MARCIE,*)*

He's a good boy.

(Beat.)

Maybe too good. . . .

A beat. MARCIE *nods off.* GEENA *dozes, too. A long moment.
Then—*

GEEN *suddenly seizes up in bed and clutches her heart.
Her eyes bulge open. The blood drains from her face. And
then—*

*She falls back down onto her pillow, her eyes still open.
Glassy. Blank.*

*Her always-puckered face relaxes. She lays there, very
still. She looks—finally—peaceful.*

SCENE 3

A few days later.

GEENA's bed is now empty, and made, tidily, with crisp hospital corners. MARCIE is the only one in the room. She lies in her bed, eyes closed, very still. We watch her for several long moments. Then—

DON enters, quietly. His demeanor has changed. Strangely, he seems almost calmer. Perhaps he holds his head a bit higher. Perhaps his spirits seem just a bit brighter. His outfit is definitely much better: he wears a pair of well-fitted pants, nice shoes, and a crisp button-down shirt under a well-tailored suit jacket, a copy of The New Yorker *stuffed into one of the pockets. The sad corduroy jacket is, thankfully, nowhere to be found.*

He looks at the empty bed where GEENA used to lie. Smiles, sadly, for just a moment. Then—

He sits down on his mother's bed. Swings his feet up slowly and lies down on the bed. In exactly the same position in which his mother used to lie. Nestles his head into the pillow. Closes his eyes.

A moment. Stillness. Then—

MARCIE

You're being creepy.

DON

(Startled.)

What?!

MARCIE

YOU'RE BEING CREEPY?

DON

Oh, sorry, I, uh . . .

He trails off. Sits up. Shakes his head; shakes the sadness away. Blinks. Straightens himself up. Then, he heads over to MARCIE*'s side of the room. Tries to sort of knock on the curtain.*

DON

(While "knocking" on the curtain.)

Ummm . . ."knock knock" . . .?

(Beat.)

MARCIE

Are you *knocking* on a curtain?

DON

Yeah. That's weird, right? I just didn't know how / else to—

MARCIE

COME *IN*, DON.

He steps onto MARCIE*'s side of the room, and stands there, looking at* MARCIE*. A beat. Then—*

DON

Hi.

MARCIE *looks at* DON.

MARCIE

Hi.

(Beat.)

MARCIE

I'm . . . sorry. About your mom.

DON

Thank you.

MARCIE

She was a good roommate.

DON

You never spoke to her. You never saw her . . .!

MARCIE

Exactly.

A beat. He smiles, a little. Then—

DON

How are you feeling?

MARCIE

I'm okay.

DON

Good.
> (Beat.)

DON

Do you need anything?

MARCIE

I'm good.

DON

Good.
> He looks around the room.

DON

Is—is Karla . . . not . . .

MARCIE

I told her to stay home today. Get some rest. Stay home forever, see if I care.

DON

Um.

MARCIE

She's no use to me if she's just sitting around here moping.

DON

Okay. / Is she—

MARCIE

She makes most things about *her*.
> (Laughs, darkly.)

That's *youth*, I suppose.
> (Ruminatively.)

The selfishness of the young artist . . .
> (With bite.)

The . . . *aspiring* artist.
> A beat. DON *deliberates. Then*—

DON
(Choosing his words carefully.)
I think—I think what happened . . . with my mother, . . . I think Karla—
(Beat.)
I think that was scary. For her. I think that was really scary.

MARCIE *shrugs.*

MARCIE
It's stupid to come to Memorial Sloan-Kettering *Cancer* Center and expect no one to *die.*

DON
Well—

MARCIE
I mean that's just willful *ignorance.*

DON
Well, I—

MARCIE
What did Karla think? That your mother was going to *live*?
(Cackles.)
Your mother looked dead the day I got here!

MARCIE *cracks herself up.*

DON
(Solemnly.)
Marcie.

MARCIE
(Sharp.)
Why are you *here*, Don.

DON *says nothing.*

MARCIE *turns her head back to the wall.* DON *looks at her.*

A beat. Then—he reaches into his pocket and pulls out an envelope, on which he has written the word "Marcie." He places it on MARCIE*'s bedstand. Then—he heads for the door. Before he can get there—*

MARCIE
I shouldn't . . . make jokes . . . like that . . .

DON *stops.*

MARCIE

I shouldn't make jokes . . . about . . . your mom. . . .

DON

Oh.

She shakes her head back and forth.

MARCIE

She was your mom.

DON

I know.

MARCIE

Now she's dead.

DON

I *know.*

MARCIE

It's not . . . *funny* . . .
A beat. Then—

DON

Yeah, it is.
A weird, huge smile overtakes DON*'s face.*

DON

I mean, it's incredibly sad, of course, and it's . . . incredibly surreal, but it's also incredibly . . . *funny*. Because . . . there's this person, right? Who you love . . . so much. And they're here, with you, every day. And then—they're just . . . *not.*
(Laughs.)
It's so weird! It's so . . . absurd . . .!
(Laughs more.)
It's . . . *so* . . . *funny* . . .!
He cracks himself up.

MARCIE

(Sharply.)
It's not funny at all.
DON *stops laughing.*

MARCIE

There's nothing less funny in the world.

(Beat.)

DON

All right.

MARCIE

What you're talking about is *relief*.

DON

Okay.

MARCIE

You think: "Oh, she's in a better place. She's out of her pain. She's moved on. And now I can, too."

(Beat.)

But you can't—*you* can't. Because *she's* in a better place, but you're not. You're *not*. . . .

(Beat.)

Because she haunts you. Inside.

(Beat.)

She makes you sick.

(Beat.)

She gives you cancer.

A beat. Then—

DON

(Gently.)

I know. That . . . you lost a daughter, Marcie.

(With aching sincerity.)

And I can't pretend to know how . . . *painful* . . . that is. But . . .

(Becoming impassioned.)

The thing is? You didn't lose your other—

MARCIE

Can you get me some fizzy water.

(Beat.)

DON

I'll get you two cups.

He leaves.

MARCIE *exhales. Takes a breath. And then—she notices the envelope on the bedstand. She reaches over, picks it up. Opens it. And takes out . . . a check.*

She studies it. Expressionless. Unblinking. Cool. Then—

She puts the check back in the envelope. Places the envelope back on the bedstand. Closes her eyes. Then—

DON *returns, carrying two Dixie cups.*

DON

I'm back . . .! Do you want me to feed them to you?

MARCIE *nods.*

DON *sits by* MARCIE *'s bed in* KARLA *'s chair. He puts one cup of seltzer down on the bedstand, then lifts the other cup to* MARCIE *'s mouth.*

DON

Okay, I'm bringing the cup of seltzer to your—

MARCIE

Don.

DON

Sorry.

DON *feeds her seltzer. She drinks.*

DON

Good . . . Good.

She drinks the whole cup.

DON *puts the empty cup on the bedstand.*

DON

Do you want the other—

MARCIE

She told you about her sister, huh.

(Beat.)

DON

She did.

MARCIE

Huh.

(Beat.)

Huh. . . . .

DON

She—

MARCIE

She never talks to me about it. She never did.

(Beat.)

DON

Well. Maybe she—

MARCIE

I'm the *mother*.

(Beat.)

I would have appreciated . . . someone to talk to.

(Beat.)

DON

I know what you mean.

MARCIE *looks at* DON. *Really takes him in.*

MARCIE

You look nice today, Don.

DON

Thank you, Marcie.

MARCIE

I like your little suit.

DON

Thank you. Thanks.

MARCIE

You usually look like a homeless person.

DON

(Laughs.)

That's what your daughter said, too . . .!

MARCIE

Huh. She said something funny. Huh.

DON *rubs his hands on his pants.*

                        DON

She's very funny, Marcie.

                        MARCIE

          (Turning to the wall.)
Uh-huh.

                        DON

She is. . . .

                        MARCIE

Hokay.
          (Beat.)

                        DON

          (Gingerly.)
I know that you two . . . have a . . . *complicated* . . . relationship. But—

                        MARCIE
          (Doing her "dead face" again.)
Blehhhggghhh!!!
          A beat. DON *just looks at* MARCIE. *Then—*

                        DON
          (Pretending that didn't just happen.)
Okay, I'm just saying that—

                        MARCIE
We don't have a "*complicated relationship.*"

                        DON

Well, okay. But—

                        MARCIE
We don't have a *relationship.*

                        DON

Okay. But—

                        MARCIE
How can you have a relationship with a person who only cares about
herself.
          (Beat.)

DON

But—she—but why do you *say* that, Marcie? She's been here with you
—every *day*. . . .

MARCIE

Because she feels like she has to.

DON

Really?

MARCIE

Because she didn't show up for me. Before.
  (Beat.)

DON

Okay.
  (Beat.)
But—

MARCIE

What?

DON

I just. Um.
  (Beat.)
My son. He, um. He came to the, ah. The . . . *funeral*. Today. And he
wore a suit . . .! I had never seen him in a suit. He didn't even wear one
to his own bar *mitzvah*. Refused to.
  (Laughs a little, remembering.)
And it wasn't, you know, an *ironic* suit. It was just . . . a suit. I didn't even
need to tell him to put it on. Neither did his mother! Apparently.
  (Beat.)
He still wouldn't *talk* to me, but. . . .
  (With a sad smile.)
He looked great.

MARCIE

So?

  A beat. DON *takes a deep breath. Then—*

DON

I just. You have to believe me, Marcie. Karla? She's. . . .

(Beat.)
She's a good person.

> MARCIE *waves her hand vaguely in* DON *'s direction.*

MARCIE
Enough.

DON
She's a . . . *generous* / person.

MARCIE
Enough.

DON
She's *not* selfish. Or, at least, not any more selfish than / the rest of us.

MARCIE
Enough!

DON
And, oh god, Marcie—she is so . . .
> *(Laughs, remembering one of* KARLA *'s jokes.)*
. . . funny . . .! / She—

MARCIE
Don. ENOUGH!

> MARCIE *turns to the wall.*

DON
> *(Softly.)*
I feel like I'm doing everything wrong.

> DON *crosses to the window. Looks out.*
> MARCIE *keeps her face turned to the wall. Then—*

MARCIE
You know. I'm funny too.
> *(Beat.)*

DON
I know.

> DON *looks at* MARCIE, *her face turned to the wall. Then—*
> MARCIE *suddenly starts to laugh.*

DON

What . . .?

MARCIE

Just remembered a joke.
>	*(Beat.)*

DON

Oh yeah?

MARCIE

A joke I used to make with my mother. When she would give me a
bath. . . .
>	*(She laughs, remembering.)*
Oh god, it's so *dumb* . . .!

DON

What is it?
>	She laughs, and turns to face DON.

MARCIE

It's—okay. Now remember I made up this joke when I was really little,
okay?

DON

Okay.

MARCIE

Here it goes: two turtles are sitting in a bathtub.

DON

Okay. . . .

MARCIE

And one turtle turns to the other turtle and says: "Can you please pass
me the soap?"

DON

Okay.

MARCIE

And the other turtle says: "What do you think I am? A typewriter?!"
>	MARCIE *cracks herself up.* DON *looks on, bewildered.*

DON

That . . . doesn't make . . . any / sense.

                              MARCIE
That's why it's *funny*.

                              DON
Oh.

    A beat. MARCIE *smiles—deep in a memory. Then—*

                              MARCIE
My mother used to *love* that joke. . . .
    (Beat, remembers.)
She used to laugh and laugh. . . .
    (Beat.)

                              DON
Oh yeah?

                              MARCIE
It was important for me. To make her laugh.
    (Beat.)

                              DON
Oh yeah . . .?

                              MARCIE
Yeah. Because otherwise. . . .
    (Beat.)

                              DON
Yeah.
    A beat. MARCIE *turns her head back to the wall. Then—*

                              MARCIE
I don't want your money.
    (Beat.)

                              DON
I know.

                              MARCIE
    (Waving her hand toward the envelope.)
Take it.

                              DON
Nope.

A beat. MARCIE*'s head stays turned to the wall.* DON *looks at the door. Then—*

MARCIE

When I found out I had cancer, do you know what I thought?
She turns to DON. *Looks right into his eyes.*

MARCIE

I thought, "Oh, thank *God.*" Because, then—this . . .
She waves her hand vaguely around her forehead, search-ing for the right word.

MARCIE

. . . *shit* . . . would be over. All. This. *Shit.* This. . . .
(Waves her hand, vaguely indicating her head.)
*Bull*shit. Up here. This—

DON

I know.

MARCIE

No, you don't.
(Laughs, darkly.)
You *don't* know.
A beat. She closes her eyes. DON *looks at* MARCIE. *Then— he crosses to her.*

DON

(Soft, but forceful.)
Do you know? How many times? I've wanted to die? In the last three months? In the last *year?* My whole life?!
He sits in KARLA*'s chair.* MARCIE *opens her eyes and looks at him.*

DON

I have *so much stuff* . . . out here—
(Indicates the outside world.)
—and so *little stuff* . . . in here—
(Indicates inside of him—his heart, soul.)
—and so much going on *up here*—
(Indicates his head.)
—that it gives me even *less* in here—
(Indicates his heart and soul, again.)

—and I—

> *A beat. He becomes overtaken with emotion. Then—*
>
> DON *picks up the envelope from the bedstand and holds it out to* MARCIE.

DON

Please, Marcie.

> MARCIE *looks at him. Then—she takes the envelope. Places it down on her bedstand. Then—*
>
> *She reaches over and opens a drawer in the bedstand. Removes a remote control. Points it toward the TV.*

DON

What are you—

MARCIE

Turning on the TV?

DON

Oh.

MARCIE

I figured we were sort of done here.
> *(Beat.)*

DON

Oh.

MARCIE

Stay and watch with me, if you want.

DON

Oh. . . .
> *(Beat.)*

Okay!

> *He sits down in* KARLA*'s chair as* MARCIE *presses a button on the remote. The TV turns on.*

VOICEOVER

"—*child-related sex crimes are considered particularly atrocious. In New York City, the hard-working detectives—*

MARCIE

> *(With a little fist pump.)*

. . . yes . . .!

99

> VOICEOVER
>
> —*who investigate these odious incidents are members of a special squad known as the SV Ped. We follow their stories."*

The episode begins. They watch TV together for a long moment. Then—

> MARCIE

I've seen this one.

MARCIE and DON*'s eyes stay glued to the screen. A long beat. The blue light flickers across* MARCIE *and* DON*'s faces as they watch TV. Then—*

KARLA enters, quietly. She sees DON*. Startles. Then—he turns and sees her.*

A beat. He takes her in. Then—

> DON

Hi Karla.

(Beat.)

> KARLA

(Uncomfortably.)

Heyyy.

*A beat. Then—*KARLA *pulls over the visitor's chair from* GEENA*'s side of the room, and joins them. They all watch TV together.*

*A long beat of this. Then—*MARCIE *eventually falls asleep.* DON *turns to* KARLA.

> DON

Um.

(With tremendous awkwardness.)

How are you?

(Beat.)

> KARLA

What?

> DON

How are—

> KARLA

I'm good.

A beat. They watch TV. Then—

DON

(Turning back to her.)

I'm good too.

(Beat.)

KARLA

(Profoundly uncomfortable.)

Cool.

A beat. They watch TV. Then—

DON

Sorry, do you think we could. . . .

KARLA

What.

DON

Idunno. Maybe we could . . . talk? Privately? For a—

KARLA

Okay.

DON *turns off the TV with the remote control. They both awkwardly stand up and head over to* GEENA*'s side of the room.*

DON

(Indicating the curtain.)

I'm just gonna . . .

KARLA

Okay.

DON *draws the curtain closed. They stand there, looking at each other. Looking away. Another beat. Then—*

DON

So. . . . How are you?

KARLA

Um.

DON

Sorry, I just asked you that.

A beat. They look at each other. Look at the floor. Then—

DON

Wow.

KARLA

What.

DON

Nothing. Just . . . you look really pretty.

KARLA

Um.

DON

Sorry. Is that . . .? Um. What I mean is. Um.
    (Beat.)
I'd like to see you again.

KARLA

You're seeing me right now.

DON

No I know, I just meant . . . like . . .

KARLA

What?

DON

I'd like to . . . go on another date.

KARLA

We did not go on a *date*, Don.

DON

No, I know. I just meant, like. . . .
    A beat. Then—he leans in to kiss her.

KARLA

What are you *doing?*

DON

Oh. Sorry.
    He pulls away.

DON

Wait why not?

KARLA

Because! This is, like . . . not the time or the *place*.

DON

Oh. Okay.

He takes a step away from her. They look at each other.
Then—

DON

Wait, sorry why not?

KARLA *lowers her voice to a whisper.* DON *does too, but*
only because that is what KARLA *is doing.*

KARLA

Because . . . my *mom* is right there? / And—

DON

Yeah, / but—

KARLA

—I don't know if she's awake or *asleep*, / and—

DON

Yeah, / but—

KARLA

—we are in a *hospital*, / and—

DON

Yeah, but—

KARLA

—it's like one in the *afternoon*, / and—

DON

Well / yeah, but—

KARLA

Your mother just died.
    (Beat.)

DON

Well. Yeah. But—

KARLA

And also I just don't know if we would actually be compatible.
Actually.
    (Beat.)

DON

   (Crushed.)
Oh really?

(Beat.)

Why not . . .?

KARLA

Idunno. 'Cause I'm a Scorpio?

DON

Um. Okay?

KARLA

And you're a Sagittarius?

DON

I'm not a Sagittarius. You made a joke about me being a Sagittarius. But I'm not a Sagittarius.

KARLA

Oh. Right. What are you?

(Beat.)

DON

(Sadly.)

I'm a Cancer.

A beat. Then—

They crack up. Then—

KARLA *suddenly moves to* DON *and hugs him. Hard. Almost knocks the wind out of him. She holds on to him for a long time. He holds on to her, too. Then—*

DON

(Still holding on to her.)

I should go.

KARLA

(Still holding on to him.)

Why?

DON

You should . . . be. With your mom.

(Beat.)

KARLA

Don't go.

He pulls away from her. Looks at her. She looks at him. Then—

He heads toward the door. Before he gets there—he stops, and turns. Looks at KARLA.

DON

I like you so much.

He leaves.

KARLA *watches him go. Then—*

She crosses to the curtain, draws it aside and enters MARCIE*'s side of the room.*

MARCIE *lies there with her eyes still closed.*

KARLA *crosses to her chair and sits. Picks up her notebook and pen and begins to scribble.*

A quiet beat. Then—

MARCIE

(Eyes still closed.)
He really likes you.
        (Beat.)

KARLA

I don't know.

MARCIE

Karla. . . .

KARLA

What?

MARCIE

You always see the negative in everything.
        (Beat.)

KARLA

I don't know. . . .

MARCIE

Ever since you were a little girl. You've had this *uncanny* ability to turn even the happiest experiences into nightmares. It's impressive, really.

KARLA

Mom—

MARCIE

"Boo hoo hoo hoo *hoo!*"

KARLA

Mom!

MARCIE

What.

KARLA

That's not . . . nice.

> *A beat.* MARCIE *turns away. Then—*

MARCIE

He *really* likes you.

> KARLA *stops scribbling.*

KARLA

He's still married.

MARCIE

Separated.

KARLA

Still. His life is a mess.

MARCIE

Whose isn't.

> *A beat.* MARCIE *lies there, eyes closed.* KARLA *returns to her notes. Then—*

MARCIE

(A tiny voice.)
Karla . . .?

> KARLA *looks at her mother and sees that* MARCIE *has started to cry.*

MARCIE

. . . I'm *scared.* . . .

> KARLA *freezes. Considers reaching .out to her mom, but stays where she is.*

KARLA

Um. Do you want anything? Some fizzy water . . .?

> MARCIE *shakes her head. And just cries. A long moment.*

Her crying is silent, but desperate. Plaintive. Painful to behold. It is the crying of someone who has not cried in a long time—the release of years and years of hardened grief.

KARLA *watches. Frozen.*

KARLA

Um.

(Beat.)

Um. . . .

A long beat. MARCIE *cries. Then—*

KARLA

Um so on my way over here? It was so funny because there was um this. Um. So I was on the 6 train?

MARCIE *starts to calm down, a bit.*

KARLA

And it was really crowded and I was just like holding onto a pole and listening to music and just kinda zoned out because I was really tired?

MARCIE *stops crying. Sniffles.*

KARLA

And um, then this, um—I had the music on *shuffle?* Which means that—

MARCIE

(Wiping her nose.)

I know what shuffle is.

KARLA

Okay cool. So I had it on shuffle, and then this, um, this . . . song came on? This song that, um. That Erika used to—do you remember? She used to play this song all the time? Really loud? Like on a loop? / In her room? It was—

MARCIE

The one about the chains?

KARLA

Yes!

MARCIE

Uch, it drove me crazy.

KARLA

I *know.*

MARCIE

The chains and the devils and the whores.

KARLA

Exactly! And my initial reaction was to be, like, oh *god*—let me switch the song, you know? 'Cause . . . Idunno, 'cause I guess when you hear a song that many times, you kind of . . . never need to hear it again?

(*Laughs.*)

And also 'cause . . . I don't know. 'Cause I guess it reminds me of . . . Erika? So.

(*Beat.*)

But then I just . . . keep listening. And then I just. Um. For some reason, I just. Like. Start crying? I mean I was standing on the subway holding onto a pole, sandwiched in between a gajillion strangers, like, *weeping.*

(*Laughs.*)

And then . . . someone taps me on the arm. And it's this total stranger —he's this short Latino dude with like these really thick glasses? And he has earbuds in, too. And he goes:

She does a gesture with her hands to indicate swapping something.

KARLA

And I'm like, "Uhhh . . . what?" And he does it again—

Does the "swapping" gesture again.

KARLA

And then he starts to take out his earbuds. And so I take out mine. And then we just . . . swap. Earbuds. And I start listening to his music and he starts listening to mine. And his music is like. . . . it's like the worst Top 40 teeny-bopper power ballad? That I have legitimately ever heard. And I'm about to take his earbuds out and be like: "Sorry dude, I can't." But then . . . I look up at him and he has *my* earbuds in and he goes:

She imitates him—big grin, bopping to the music, giving a thumbs up sign.

KARLA

And I go:

She does the same thing—smiles big, bops to the music and gives a thumbs up sign.

KARLA

And Mom? We rode the train like that? For *half an hour.*

(Beat; remembers.)

And then the train stops at 59th Street, and I realize that I have to get off at the next stop. So I start taking out his earbuds and he takes out mine—and we have said literally *not one* word to each other this entire time—and I give him back his earbuds and he gives me back mine. And the train slows down, and I'm about to get off, and I look at the guy, to be like, "Bye?" And he just . . . puts his hand on my shoulder.

(Beat.)

And he says . . . nothing. He just . . . looks at me. With his hand on my shoulder. And I look at him. And then . . .

(Beat.)

I get off the train.

A beat. KARLA *becomes lost in a thought. She smiles, remembering. Then—she turns and sees that* MARCIE's *eyes are closed.*

KARLA

Oh.

KARLA *returns to her notebook.*

A beat. Stillness.

KARLA *scribbles and* MARCIE *lies there, eyes closed. Then—*

MARCIE

Read to me.

KARLA

What?

MARCIE *waves her hand toward* KARLA's *notebook.*

MARCIE

Read me your jokes. Your new bits.

(Beat.)

KARLA

Really . . .?

MARCIE *nods, eyes still closed.*

KARLA

Um.

A beat. Then—KARLA *flips to a page, and begins to read.*

KARLA

"I've been single for so long? I've started having wet dreams about my vibrator."

A beat. Then—MARCIE *chuckles.*

MARCIE

That's funny.

KARLA

You think . . .?

MARCIE *nods.*

KARLA

Do you think it should be "wet dreams" or "sex dreams"?

MARCIE

"Wet dreams." Definitely.

KARLA *beams.*

KARLA

Thanks. Me too.

KARLA *turns the page.*

KARLA

'K how 'bout this: "Instead of a strong, chiseled, oiled-up man throwing open my bedroom door and raping me? I just have visions of like, my vibrator standing in the archway, backlit by silvery moonlight, some-times wearing a fedora (sometimes not), and lovingly fucking me 'til sunrise."

MARCIE *cackles.*

KARLA

(Glowing.)
You *like* that . . .?

MARCIE

That's great . . .!

KARLA

Really . . .?!

MARCIE

That's *funny*. . . .

KARLA

Do you think the rape part is too much?

MARCIE

(Shakes her head, eyes still closed.)

No. It's awesome.

KARLA *'s eyes mist up.*

KARLA

Really, Mom . . .?

(Beat.)

MARCIE

You're *funny*, Karla. . . .

KARLA *'s eyes fill with tears.*

KARLA

Thanks, Mom.

MARCIE

You're a funny girl.

MARCIE *reaches out for* KARLA *'s hand, and* KARLA *takes it.*

MARCIE

You're a good girl.

KARLA *begins to cry.*

KARLA

Thanks, Mom. Thanks.

MARCIE

You're a funny, funny girl, ...

The two women hold hands.

MARCIE *opens her eyes, and squeezes* KARLA *'s hand.* KARLA
cries, and squeezes it back.

Blackout.

END OF PLAY.